ENDANGERED TIGER

A Community Under Threat

NEIL M. C. SINCLAIR

ENDANGERED TIGER
A Community Under Threat

ISBN 1-898317-09-7

Typeset by Dragon & Tiger Enterprises
Cover Design by Malin Flynn
Rear Cover Photograph by John McKernan
Tiger Bay Skyline Illustration by Neil Sinclair
Printed by Zenith Media
Published by Butetown History & Arts Centre
with the assistance of Leslie Clarke &
a "Connecting Communities" grant from the Home Office

DEDICATION

To my loving mother
Beatrice A. Headley-Sinclair
(1909 - 2001)

ACKNOWLEDGEMENTS

I extend my thanks to the people of old Tiger Bay and the Docks, both home and abroad, and to the staff and volunteers at BHAC whose being made this book possible. Particularly to Tony Lewis whose indefatigable efforts helped to organise the photographs which gave faces and identity to many of the characters and places mentioned in this book. Also to Julia Young whose encouragement is much appreciated and archivist Molly Maher. In addition I thank Dr. Lauri Ramey of Cardiff University whose editorial suggestions inspired me to reorganize many sections of the manuscript and refine its content. And for his expert editing and proof reading of the final draft, a special thank you goes to Glenn Jordan. Last but not least I cannot overlook the support and strength I receive from my sister Leslie Clarke and all my family, but ultimately I thank the Power Most High without whom no creative potential is possible.

CONTENTS

ENDANGERED TIGER

PREFACE

"... one thing the knockers never give it credit for
was its heart. Tiger Bay had heart."

Dorothy Hendrickson

Delving into the intimate past has its pitfalls and some may question what gives me the right to expose to the light of day aspects of the life and times of people in old Tiger Bay. To answer this I can only say that I have deep abiding respect for the people of this much maligned community, which in essence inspires me to write about it. Furthermore, what was so conspicuous about *The Tiger Bay Story* after its publication by *Butetown History & Arts* in 1993, was the dearth of many characters and events I assumed I had included. For although such thoughts reverberated through my mind at the time I composed that manuscript, I clearly failed to write them down. This engendered a need to continue documenting the history of a community whose elders, the repositories of such a wealth of information, were and are steadily passing away. Like so many others in the community, I have attended the Alice Street Mosque, St Paul's, St Cuthbert's and St Mary's Churches so regularly in the last decade that we have become, as it were, "professional mourners."

When members of respected families make their final departure from Tiger Bay St. Mary's Church is filled to the rafters and part of the congregation is forced to remain outside in all weathers. With them so many stories are going to the grave forever. Thus the idea that the original Tiger Bay community will be lost from memory is the main driving force that motivates me to document its history, particularly now that residents themselves are beginning to agree with media commentaries that Tiger Bay is a thing of the past.

"The Bay's finished. It's been finished for years now," commented local resident Charmaine Taylor, one brilliant late summer day in the year 2000.

"Mind you," she continued encouragingly, "it was still *happening* when I first came to live here 30 years ago."

Typical mid-1930s Tiger Bay gathering enjoying the pleasures of Loudoun Square Park. Among the group can be found: Gracie Johnson; Johnnie Silva; Merced Ali; Harry & Georgie Ernest; Oliver Fernandez; Shirley Hassan; Margaret Freeman; Peter Brito; Donnie Graham; Willy Sweeton (Black Dolly's son); Beresford Grant; Raymond Fettah & Patti Lima. The old-fashioned lamppost and railings still in place until the Second World War run along the east side of the square.
(Photo courtesy of BHAC)

Since the mid-1900s the decline of the industrial docks over the last 30 years or more has been well documented in the South Wales Press and this decline has clearly had an impact on local residents, not to say the rest of South Wales.

Tiger Bay, or North Butetown for the uninitiated, in particular has been allowed to deteriorate and disintegrate while South Butetown has undergone a transmutation into a magnificent showpiece waterfront. To use the phrase coined by the Public Relations department of the Development Corporation, it is now "Europe's most exciting waterfront development." On the other hand, the Docks, the original community of South Butetown, like its counterpart in rapidly deteriorating Tiger Bay, has been well-nigh marginalised out of existence.[1] Moreover, local people, despite the promise of the developments surrounding the community, feel disenfranchised and not surprisingly their view of the future is at times extremely pessimistic.

Endangered Tiger attempts to document the social decline that began with the dispersal of many of its residents as a result of the 1960s demolition of the community. It is my wish that *Endangered Tiger* might give to the people who lived in the dockland a sense of pride and to those who did not an understanding of one of Cardiff's most misunderstood communities. And perhaps such an appreciative understanding cannot be more eloquently expressed than it was one hundred years ago in 1902 in the following poem from the pen of M which appeared one Saturday in the August 23rd edition of the *Western Mail*:

Sweet Tiger Bay

By land and water, through toil and batter,
I've spent — no matter how many years;
But pleasant places and pretty faces
Still reconcile me to this vale of tears;
Have no memorial either grand or gay
That can outshine thee, as I outline thee
On memory's tablets, sweet Tiger Bay!
Oh Bay of Beauty! My pleasing duty
Is to salute thee in a frenzy fine,
For whose exalting in verse unhalting
I bow to Phœbus and the Muses nine;
If my devotion with equal potion
From far-famed helicon they do repay,
I'll straightway tune a verse which through
the Universe
Will waft thy praises, sweet Tiger Bay!

The Bay of Rio hath got a trio,
Earth, sea, and sky, oh! surpassing fair,
And thine, oh Naples! with beauty staples
Th' aesthetic pilgrim's admiration there;
The Bay of Sydney to artists' kidney
Hath prov'd a tickler in a wondrous way —
But all their grandeur I'd freely squander
One night to wander in sweet Tiger Bay!

Here all dominions, races and opinions
Have many precious specimens on view,
Maltese and Arab, German, Jew, and Carrib —
The meek Hibernian and the mad Hindoo;
Whatever ritual is their habitual,
Whatever politics their passions sway,
They're all believers in pints and sleevers,
When once they're anchor'd in
sweet Tiger Bay!

These gentle jokers, with tongs and pokers,
Sometimes make music in that striking style
Which dyes your cranium like a red geranium
And makes you dance but never makes you smile;
And sometimes sirens, with their smoothing irons,
Charm these environs with that winsome play

Which makes a mockery of glass and crockery,
And with a rockery strews Tiger Bay!

With names well-chosen thy streets would cozen
Hearts almost frozen to admire and love,
Sweet Angelina and dear Christina
Salute the glad beholder from above!
And fair Maria and gay Sophia
Invite the love-lorn mariner to stay,
While Peel and Nelson fling martial spells on
The Imperial denizens of Tiger Bay!
Ye blissful bowers! in my boyhood's hours
I cull'd choice flowers —
of speech within your shade;
And play'd like curlew in that classic purlieu
Which mortals meanly call "Canal Parade";
When manhood found me new pleasures
crowned me,
The morning "sleever" and the midnight fray —
Gods! What a blender of Grace and Splendour
Of the True and Tender is Tiger Bay!

With age o'ertaking me, and friends forsaking me,
And debts – to name them all I'd hardly dare —
I live in troubles, but they pass like bubbles,
When Fancy conjures up the days that were:
Put Death before me, and an Angel o'er me,
To bear me upward-this to him I'd say:
"Young friend, your attitude has won my gratitude;
But please, another night in Tiger Bay!"

Chapter One

ENDANGERED TIGER

For me 1999 proved to be a year of major setbacks both personally and politically. In the May council elections Plaid Cymru nominated me as their candidate for the Butetown Ward. But as Betty Campbell, MBE also chose to run, upon early retirement as headmistress of Mount Stuart Primary School, it proved to be a tough race for the hearts of the people as she emerged and the winning independent candidate. Non-resident Labour Party representative Mohamed Javed took second place. My feelings about Plaid Cymru's third place were somewhat assuaged by the sincere congratulations I received outside the City Hall for running a dignified campaign from staunch members of the Labour Party Idda Mohamed and her sisters Halima and Miriam of West Close. In any event, had I won the contest, it would have proved a pyrrhic victory, as, in the immediate aftermath of the election I collapsed with fatigue and was eventually hospitalised at the Llandough and Heath Hospitals two months later.

Being over a period of a few years chair of Multicultural Crossroads, a member of the board of the then Race Equality Council, chair of both the Norwegian Church management committee and the Horn of Africa Charity, vice-chair of Butetown History & Arts Centre and editor of its magazine *The Voice of the Tiger*, member of the Waterfront Partners Group, Cardiff Bay Business Forum, the now defunct Cardiff Bay Community Trust and sole proprietor of Dragon & Tiger Enterprises clearly had its price. In retrospect I can see the folly of voluntarily taking on too many responsible positions in local community groups. Loss of consciousness on two occasions was the unanticipated cost of such excessive involvement and a confrontation with the possibility of a premature death. Were it not for the outstanding efforts of the medical staff at the University Hospital of Wales I would not have survived to write this book. But the reason I introduce this sorry episode of my life here is solely because of a very unusual experience I underwent during the worst part of my illness. Some of the medication I was given was prone to induce hallucinations. Thus the account which follows could potentially be explained away by this fact. But I am not convinced by such scientific skepticism. All I know is that whilst in excruciating pain alone in a solitary hospital room laying prostrate on a bed I looked up to see a women peering down at me. Although her mouth moved as if articulating something, I did not hear any words but that she was my mother's mother Agnes seemed uncannily certain. She was only there for a fleeting moment before the sudden appearance of two trilby wearing black gentlemen, dressed in well tailored overcoats, obscured her departure.

The life-like presence of these men in this startling visitation, who were also gazing down at my wretched condition, raised a dour sensation of foreboding and consternation as to who they were. As their visit immediately followed that of my grandmother, perhaps were they my maternal and paternal grandfathers. If so, had they come to ease my journey across the great divide or was this merely a conjuring trick of a delirious mind?

As these were people who had died many years before my birth, the medication's hallucinatory influence as a possible cause for these apparitions was all the more disturbing. Yet notwithstanding the fact that photographs of them were in family albums, the conjuring up of still photographic memories is somehow far too simple an explanation for the animated movement of their visitation at such a critical juncture in my life.

Besides these ethereal visitors, many real world people from the community I had known from my childhood days growing up in the old Tiger Bay also made regular visits during my two months hospital stay — in addition to members of my immediate family. Given the circumstances, quite naturally I told my sister about these apparitions. Together Leslie and I wondered why our father's mother Margaret Helen had not also made an appearance. Reflecting on this raised the spectre of my mother's uncle Ethelbert. Perhaps he was the other gentleman and not my grandfather Danny Sinclair whom I had originally presumed. This further raised the possibility that they were not there to help me across but concerned that I should survive to look after Beatrice, their then 90 year old daughter and niece, my mother.

I made no bones to Lesley about the physicality of the presence of our deceased relatives and clearly my sincerity evoked memories of her own about her first encounter with the possibility of the other world which involved an incident that took place in 1939 when she was only five years old. We lived at that time — I say "we" but I was yet to be born in 1944 — at 19 Frances Street, which I had occasion to mention in my book *The Tiger Bay Story*. Desperate to go to the loo, Leslie had had to make a journey from the living room along the narrow passage to the kitchen where an emergency bucket could be found to save the family from going down the garden path in the cold dead of night. Usually Mam left a lighted candle in the kitchen but when Lesley entered the passage that night everything was absolutely pitch black. The candle had gone out and in the intense darkness of that moment the strangest thing occurred. Approaching her from the kitchen was a little boy. Since she could see nothing else, her infant mind wondered how this could be and where the unfamiliar

My mother Beatrice Headley at the age of 18 in 1927.
(*Photo courtesy of the Sinclair family*)

child had come from. Being only five she was unaware of the possibility of ghosts or any other such phenomena making such realistic appearances. Alarmed by his presence but still desperately needing to go to the loo, she rushed back into the living room telling Mam to light the way making no mention of the boy.

At eleven years of age, however, she recognised the little boy she had seen in the passage in a family album. The boy had been our brother Leonard who had died at two years of age.

Provoked by this revelation, my mother revealed to Lesley an incident she had experienced when she had been a child living on Somerset Street in Grangetown. An elderly woman dressed in dark, old fashioned clothes came into her bedroom.

"Do you want to go with me?" the kindly woman asked.

When she described this woman to her mother my grandmother recognized her as her own mother Margaret, my mother's Lancashire grandmother. Obviously, as I am here to reflect upon these frail glimpses of posthumous communication, my mother *did not go* with her. But I had never actually known my grandmother in my lifetime so naturally seeing the apparition of her and the two black gentlemen at the side of my sick bed intimated the possibility that I was close to the end of my life. Those thoughts, of course, were premature. Clearly, the thought of my predeceasing mama was anathema to them. I had to get out of this hospital. I was needed in Loudoun Square to see that her last days were comfortable ones in what remained of the moribund Tiger Bay she had known. Thus the danger of approaching death had to bide its time for me. It nevertheless continued to stretch out its clutching hands towards the once vibrant and exciting community near the sea where I had the good fortune to be born. Like the ghosts that clung to my past, the last vestiges of my Tiger Bay home struggle to remain. Having been caged between the Great Western Railway built in the 1850s and the Bristol Channel at its southern shoreline the vital force of that once proud Tiger now cowers at the desperate point of extinction.

During the many moments I was alone recuperating in my hospital room in the Heath, I often stared out of the window toward the sea which swept up on the shore of my native community. That I came to love that place so well has as much to do with the family of the Countess of Loudoun as with my own. Although still retaining her family name, Countess Flora of Loudoun must be rolling in her Ayreshire grave at the sight of the continuing decay of the once grand square that stands at the heart of what remains of the old Tiger Bay community.

She and her husband the First Marquis of Hastings must have cringed in horror at the 1960s demolition of Sophia Street, named in honour of their daughter the Marchioness of Bute, particularly after Sophia's husband John, the Second Marquis of Bute, the man most instrumental in the rise of Cardiff's coal port, had determined that many streets in the residential community of the industrial dockland would maintain the names of Bute family members for time immemorial. Or so it was thought. But already the memory of *So-Fire*, as the old Tiger Bay Sophia Street was pronounced, has faded from the minds of the current generation of Butetown inhabitants. The Marquis initiated the building of Butetown as the home of the well-to-do of his day. Is it possible that this John, who "was active in the agitation against slavery and in gathering information on the consequences of its abolition,"[1] was also aware that he was laying the foundation of what was to become one of Britain's most well known multi-ethnic communities? One can only wonder. Yet, although it is believed to have vanished in the 1990s, in the wake of a glamorous Cardiff Bay tidal wave, the community lingers on, despite council deprivation and media efforts to instill the idea that Tiger Bay no longer exists.

Identifying Butetown as "the most deprived ward in Cardiff," an article entitled "Welsh Areas Reach Depths of Deprivation" appeared in the 24 August 2000 edition of the *South Wales Echo*. It indicated that Butetown "… ranked 37th on the overall list" of poverty for Wales. Published by the Welsh National Assembly, these details came from the *Welsh Index of Multiple Deprivation 2000* report of August 2000. However, subsumed under the Butetown ward are many brown field sites which have been transformed into new residential communities as part of the redevelopment. Their values range from £50,000 to half a million pounds. Yet despite twelve years of regeneration, orchestrated by the Cardiff Bay Development Corporation, the community of Tiger Bay and the Docks, the original residential areas known as Butetown, still maintains the ranking of most deprived ward in Cardiff. Clearly, were it not for the new residential developments of Adventurers Quay and Century Wharf, it would still register as the primary area of deprivation in the whole of Wales.

That the inhabitants of Tiger Bay and the Docks have been excluded and ignored by Cardiff's council is historical fact as far as locals are concerned, and indicates nothing new. Yet, despite the adversities of neglect which existed long before the 1948 arrival of the *S.S. Empire Windrush*, which ignited the *multiculturalisation* in much of the United Kingdom, the community, sustained by the prowling vital force of the Tiger, determined that it would survive regardless. Even though a Butetown/Grangetown Strategy is presently afoot, Butetown, continuing its decline under the jurisdiction of the newly created Cardiff County Council, flounders into dilapidation and disrepair while surrounded by trendy new housing and office developments.

In horrified response to an article which appeared in the Tuesday 5 September 2000 edition of the *South Wales Echo* describing the plight of George and Dora Desmond, local resident Peggy Farrugia, had cause to state that she was once proud to say "I was born and bred in Tiger Bay." This elderly couple, two life long residents of the Docks area, who engendered Peggy's sympathy, had been plagued by nocturnal disturbances from unruly youths who had taken after dark control of the hallways in the maisonette side of Angelina Street where they resided. Although Peggy was rightfully upset by the cowardly behaviour of these youths towards the Desmonds, many of these youngsters do not even reside in the community.

Not only the Desmonds but many other residents are overwhelmed by these nocturnal disturbances which are encouraging many to want to leave the area for the first time, as did Sylvia, wife to the late Ossie Abrams, during the summer of 2000.

"I love my Docks," said Sylvia to one of her neighbours, "but I have to get away." Poignantly the family pet dog had to be restrained as he kept jumping out of the car that was moving Sylvia to the distant suburb of St Mellons.

Other residents of Angelina Street, like Jennifer Herbert, prefer to stay at the homes of nearby relatives, rather than share accommodation with the field mice and cockroaches currently infesting their properties. Thus, as the area descends into apparent slum conditions, there is a certain irony in the current social decline and physical disintegration that is driving long-term residents away from the community in which they have spent their lifetime. Built less that 40 years ago to replace housing defined to be in a state of slum condition by city authorities, these, dare it be said, "ugly" grey-brick maisonettes failed the test of longevity the earlier structures enjoyed.

"Those old houses were strong, man!" said local Bay Boy Terry Bishop who assisted in the demolition. In many cases he confirmed the old structures required nine strikes of the wrecking ball before they fell.

Granted the odd property here and there was in a state of

disrepair, I nevertheless find it necessary to disagree with the findings that described old Tiger Bay as a slum. The word "slum," one not used by those who lived there, is an uptown utterance. Loudoun Square, for example, was spacious and tranquil, with trees that would rival those of the Hayes today. If it had been refurbished and still existed, it would be no exaggeration to say it would equal the likes of Berkeley Square and Russell Square in London.

Ominously co-existing with the late 1980s and early 1990s regeneration project has been a growing pessimism on the part of its residents. The local paranoia that the recent regeneration, coordinated by Cardiff Bay Development

East view of Georgian side of old Loudoun Square, circa 1954. (Photo courtesy of Olwen Watkins)

Corporation, was undertaken without them in mind, is becoming the most dangerous threat to the continued existence of the community.

With the apparent object of bringing about its total eradication, by defining our community as a slum, the Housing Authority accomplished the utter destruction of the architectural legacy which was the inspiration of the Second Marquis of

Bute. The orderly streets, parks and lanes conducive to social communication laid out in the first quarter of the 19th century all vanished, only to be replaced by mismatched streets and empty, architecturally unimaginative concrete squares such as West Close once was, and the two ends of Christina Street continue to be.

Originally built for the affluent of the 19th century, many of the houses in the community, therefore, were of a grand, if not elegant style like the ones that still exist in Bute Crescent, where the Eli Jenkins Pub is found today. In fact, this was the area that began the expansion of Cardiff from a village into the city it is today. Admittedly, compared to the Georgian style homes of Loudoun Square or Flemish gabled, Victorian and Edwardian buildings of other streets, the house my grandfather bought, and in which I was born in 1944, was one of the more modest terraced houses. In fact, as if purposely to taunt surviving members of old Tiger Bay and the Docks, who were powerless to stop compulsory purchase orders on their homesteads in the early 1960s, dwellings similar in structure to the more modest houses found in the old community that were later demolished still stand in Splott, Roath and Canton and other parts of Cardiff. Such preserved instances of old structures raise the question: If they are still here, what was *really* wrong with our homes?

In the 1950s, Tiger Bay was visited by the late Archbishop Trevor Huddleston, who had previously been resident in apartheid South Africa where Sophia Town, a community not dissimilar in its multi-ethnic makeup to Tiger Bay, was being forcibly obliterated in the interests of a racist policy of segregation. Had it not been for the *South Wales Echo*, this visit may have remained a faded memory. A photograph of the event reemerged in the *Local News Section* of the April 22, 1998 edition. The picture, taken outside the Marchioness of Bute on Sophia Street, also included two of the most well-loved priests in Tiger Bay at the time: Father Oman and Father Bradley of St Mary the Virgin Church.

Journalist Amanda Baillie included in her article the Archbishop's comment that Tiger Bay *was a paradise compared to the slums of South Africa.* However, her remark that the area was "once known as Tiger Bay" was clearly an unintentional offence to many like myself who still go to sleep every night in Tiger Bay. Of course, as an outsider and with the emphasis placed on the name Butetown by the authorities, it is not surprising that this reporter believed local people to have abandoned the name "Tiger Bay" in favour of "Butetown." By the

(L to R) Fr Oman, other church members & Beatrice Sinclair.
(Photo courtesy of the Sinclair family)

close of the 1950s Tiger Bay had experienced 150 years of stability and social familiarity. However, all that was to change with the onset of the 1960s.

In his unpublished 1990 Bachelor's thesis *From Tiger Bay … to Cardiff Bay — 150 Years of Socio-Economic Change in Butetown*, local resident Neil Sullivan stated:

> In the 1960's the area was almost totally redeveloped with public housing, with the intention of removing not only the original buildings but also the stigma attached to the area. This crude attempt at social engineering was however unsuccessful, shattering a community structure which had evolved over generations and causing yet another 'problem' estate to be built.[2]

The "stigma attached to the area" that Sullivan's dissertation refers to will be taken up in the next chapter, but the current decline of our community can be traced back to its initial "shattering," brought about by the unsuccessful and crude attempt at social engineering begun in the 1960s. Representative of local reaction to this forced dispersal from the community was Olwen Watkin's remark, when told she had to go: "I don't have to got to anything! I am not a cow or a cat. You can't tell me I've *got to* get out!" We shall meet Olwen once again in Chapter Eleven entitled *The First Blow — What The Demolition Did.*

In the meantime, ending an era stretching back to the eighteen century, former racing car driver Johnny Dumfries, the Seventh Marquis of Bute, severed the Bute family link with Cardiff Castle in 1997. Thus, at the beginning of the new millennium, connected to the Bute family in name only, the *problem estate* is about to undergo another regeneration. Irrespective of the potential upheaval, many residents of Angelina Street still want to be rehoused within the confines of the community, despite having become increasingly fed up with the deterioration and collective depression this turmoil has aroused. Furthermore, many want to return to Angelina Street after its redevelopment. Famous for its pubs, like the Bute and Marchioness of Bute and outdoor gambling casino, Angelina Street was a vibrant street. Birth place of famous sportsmen like Billy Boston and Joey Erskine, it was the show of life. You simply had to stroll down the pavements of this terraced street to see what was going on, even if your journey was shorter along Canal Parade or Bute Street. However, the decision by the Housing Authority to demolish the west side of the post-development version of the street was made several years ago. Some residents, now tired of undermined expectations, have opted to move, albeit reluctantly, from the area altogether.

Currently the community structure is suffering another devastating blow but the Tiger is not yet extinct. Thus, with our future as a community endangered, should we not look back into the community's historical legacy to strengthen our resolve, regain our community's built-in resilience and determine what is at stake for the Tiger. We should not assist the mechanism of social engineering by inadvertently colluding with our detractors and bring about the total decimation and transformation of our area into a high priced *des res* for outsiders who have no historical connection with the area at all.

Chapter Two

THAT REPUTATION

In the 24 June 1989 edition of the *South Wales Echo*, Dorothy Hendrickson, the eldest sister of rugby legend Billy Boston, MBE, described Tiger Bay as:

> a rough, tough, sometimes violent area. Part poor, part middle-class with people of every creed, nationality and religion.

However football hooliganism and the daily barrage of violence shown in the media today would make the violence attributed to old Tiger Bay pale into insignificance. Like Dorothy and so many other community minded residents before me, as a native son I have also submitted a number of responses to the local press in an attempt to rectify misrepresentations of our past. As did Tiger Bay's Manuel Delgado, the first black solicitor in Wales, when he expressed his astonishment at the prejudice found in "some of the things Jack Jones" stated in the *South Wales Echo* of 20 June 1967 referring to "the people originally in Butetown as being the flotsam and jetsam of the seven seas" who are "trying to prove themselves worthy of integration."

Thus, it would be remiss of me if I failed to consider the negative reputation that the name Tiger Bay has conjured throughout South Wales in the twentieth century, particularly as we have begun the new millennium. Local journalists, rarely providing dates for the alleged dreaded days of *ill-repute*, continue to foster this altogether undeserved and disparaging reputation. It is amazing that the ports of the world still recall the grand hospitality received among the people of old Tiger Bay, while local historians at times failed to even notice it. Although the occasional café on Bute Street, which offered a more salacious menu in the secluded recesses of its back rooms, can lay claim to a sordid past, the vast majority of streets in the area had a long tradition of respectable seagoing working class families who contributed to the wealth that built this city.

"I have heard tell of what a terrible place Tiger Bay was a long time ago," begins an extract in Beatrice Sinclair's *Time to Go*. This unpublished memoir of a ninety-year-old resident of the area, which was placed in the *South Glamorgan Archive* several years ago, goes on to say:

> [B]ut I know nothing of this and can only speak of the Tiger Bay I know. Of the open doors at Christmas and New Year. Of the band of players visiting each house in turn that wanted them to enter. Of the funerals that were like a state occasion. One old man in top hat and frock-coat led every one, with dozens of walkers who would walk in front until they came to Kingsway and then ride on to the cemetery.

Seen through the eyes of a native of Tiger Bay, her account paints a different picture, which sharply contrasts with negative images and shows:

> How very different was life when I grew up and got married to the son of a Barbadian like my father. The children of my father's countrymen, and all the others whom he'd disliked so, went to school together, played together, grew up together and to see so many many nationalities living in such harmony should have been a lesson to the world.

While most of the men were employed at sea, the community was full of industrious people, like Lillian Constance Reeves or Kitty "Said" (pronounced "Side") Mohammed, who ran registered seamen's Boarding Houses on Patrick and Peel street, respectively. The efforts of the hard working members of this community far outweighed the activities which took place in a few dubious cafés on old Bute Street or on the docks, such as smuggling contraband and shipboard prostitution.

Thus, having crossed the threshold of the new millennium, we need once and for all to go straight to the crux of this matter. Yes, Tiger Bay had a bad name, but why? If the abject racism that was prevalent in Wales at the turn of the twentieth century, and described later in this chapter, is combined with the fact that the largest population of Africans to be found anywhere in Wales was located in and around Loudoun Square, then it is not difficult to conjecture the source of its origin. Clearly there is something disingenuous about this self-perpetuating, negative myth of Tiger Bay, engendered perhaps out of a psychological need to suppress the kind of open racism Lord Callaghan mentions in Chapter Six, *Off Limits*. Whether they were West Africans or East African Somalis, these were seamen whose toil and effort helped make Cardiff rich and affluent.

When ashore, the majority of these men were perfect gentlemen, always smartly dressed, carrying walking canes and wearing top hats which were doffed to passers-by. But who

Some of the Africans and West Indians who lived in Tiger Bay at the turn of the Twentieth Century. Pictured among the group with Rev Stanley Watson of Loudoun Square's Wesleyan Chapel are African seaman Joe Brown of South Loudoun Place standing directly behind Rev Watson and Barbadian seaman Walter St Clair of old Loudoun Square, seated front row left.
(Photo courtesy of P G Kernick)

knew what Africans did after dark? By this time stories of the criminal violence perpetrated by black men were legendary. For example the Tuesday, 22 January 1918, edition of the *Western Mail* ran the headline DANGEROUS NEGRO RUNS AMOK AT CARDIFF above a story that proclaimed:

> A negro who ran amok at Cardiff Great Western Railway Station on Thursday last was sentenced on Monday to six months' hard labour for assaulting Police Constable Joseph Reed, a second sentence for assaulting Railway-constable Charles Creel being ruled to run concurrently.
>
> A further charge of obstructing Railway-detective Beynon was considered in passing sentence.
>
> Mr. W. H. Davies (Prosecuting for the Great Western Railway Company) said defendant issued from a cloak-room at 5:30 p.m. with an open clasp-knife in his hand, and threatened to rip open anybody who came near him. Police constable Reed appeared on the scene and quickly closed with the defendant and disarmed him. A most violent struggle followed. Police Constable Creel and Detective Beynon threw themselves into the struggle, defendant hitting out at all three, and he was only got to the police station with the greatest difficulty.
>
> Defendant: You all want to hang a poor negro this morning.

With the main purpose of identifying his violent nature, this article helps to recreate the mood of those times. Undoubtedly in today's press the anonymous black man would have his name published, whereas during the year that saw the catastrophic First World War come to an end, it clearly was not deemed necessary to name him. Thus to outsiders he was the "Boogeyman" and in some affluent homes in Cardiff, he was the threat used to get recalcitrant children off to bed. "I'll take you down to Loudoun Square and leave you there!" was enough to get them safely tucked in. So goes a humorous anecdote from Stuart Neal, a descendant of the Neal & West Company which operated in Cardiff Docks. However, working hard to defend and raise good families, these Africans left Cardiff a great legacy by producing a number of world famous personalities. The father of the international chanteuse Shirley Bassey was Calibar from Nigeria, Ryan Giggs's great grandfathers and Billy Boston's father were Mende and Soso, respectively, from the West African country of Sierra Leone.

Those challenging incidents that Tiger Bay people had to endure had become folklore throughout the community by the time I was a lad and even today any number of people still living, like Charlie Waith and Donald John, can vividly recount those years. As independent Councillor, Betty Campbell, MBE recently confided she had read aloud my mother's childhood experience of the 1919 race riots to conference members of a Commission for Racial Equality gathering held in Llandrindod Wells in the late summer of 2000.

"Is that lady still living?" asked one of the fascinated listeners after hearing this account.

"She was playing bingo in the community centre last Sunday!" Betty replied.

My mother's childhood experience of the 1919 race riots was told at some length in Chapter Two of *The Tiger Bay Story*. Referring to those times, the 19 June 1919 *Echo* reported the incident, without identifying the victims by name as in the case of the *Dangerous Negro* who ran amok:

> A mob of one thousand men (sic) attacked the homes of
> two negroes.

Never letting anyone forget that fear-inspiring incident which took place on Somerset Street in Grangetown, Trinidadian-born Joseph Friday, who fortunately lived to a ripe old age, was one of those "negroes." The other was my grandfather James Augustus Headley, who had recently received gold and bronze medals from King George for his bravery at sea. To save his life he was forced to flee from his home in the land he had just defended. Thwarted in their attempt to catch him at home, some of the men among the mob still beat up my grandmother Agnes and ransacked her home, smashing the furniture and all her cherished china ornaments. My mam, who was nine at the time, was left unharmed but says her mother never got over the trauma of seeing her cosy home destroyed.

"That's what you get for marrying a black man," said the policeman to my grandmother — adding insult to injury after arriving a day later to make inquiries.[1]

These distressing events precipitated my grandfather's decision to leave and eventually buy a house in the Bay, where it was safer, because these same cowardly rioters, some in British Army uniform, were warned by the police not to try to enter Tiger Bay. The Africans they were told had built an arsenal and would defend themselves, so any bloodshed in the area would not just be theirs. The entire multi-ethnic community stood together to fight off the rioters who rode down Bute Street on horseback. Chinese shopkeepers played their part by supplying pepper to local defenders to throw into the eyes of the horses. As they reared up, the riders were disloged and easily dispensed with, once on foot. Even so, rocks hailed down from the Taff Vale Railway embankment, as certain rioters, not daring to stand in Bute Street itself, threw stones at people below from their safe vantage point above. A few people still living can provide anecdotes or give

Beatrice Headley dressed for her confirmation at age 7 just two years before her terrifying ordeal during the 1919 riots.
(Photo courtesy of the Sinclair family)

their version of those turbulent days. Of course, it was the people of colour who lived outside Tiger Bay who suffered most, my maternal grandfather being one example.

As the Chinese formed an integral part of the multi-ethnic community that was Tiger Bay and the Docks, we must not forget them. After all, they were the first non-Europeans to settle in the area and they also had their troubles. Although only allowed to run restaurants and laundries, they were nevertheless a very industrious people. The Chinese laundry on Bute Street at the corner of Hodges Row is often remembered. Housewives like Hilda Mary Jemmett or Clare, the English wife of Igbo seaman Jeremiah Mbakwe, often had their husbands' shirts done by that laundry. Mrs Mbakwe's youngest son Chuku was often sent from their home on Evelyn Street down the Docks to the laundry to get them. After writing notes in Chinese on a piece of paper, the man would tear it in two. This was the ticket. This busy man, who was always on his own in the shop when Chuku arrived, washed, ironed and starched the clothes by hand before wrapping them in brown paper when finished.

"No tickee, no washee!" was the sharp and abrupt response Chuku would hear if he came without the torn half of that piece of paper.

Notwithstanding the economic constraints, the Chinese prospered despite the odds and branched out into other parts of the town. However, 1911 brought the Anti-Chinese rioters who smashed up their businesses, forcing the Chinese back into Tiger Bay, where most of them re-established shops and restaurants along Bute Street, amidst the Jewish business community, remaining there well into the late 1950s. In fact Mr Wing's *Sam On Yen*, the first Chinese restaurant in Wales, was still in existence at the time of the ill-conceived demolition in the early 1960s of our "very wonderful community." Incidentally, Nora Glagow recalled childhood memories of how she often ran errands for "Auntie Ada," Mr Wing's wife.

Including, it appears, the obtaining of her surreptitious bottle of gin, hidden in a brown paper bag so that her husband would not

Mr Wing & Florence Austin in the kitchen of the Sam On Yen Chinese restaurant, the first of its kind in Wales.
(Photo courtesy of Hulton Getty)

know. Another of Nora's odd, and seemingly morbid, recollections about those early days, when she visited the Wing home above the restaurant, was her discovery of an ornate oriental coffin that stood upright in their living room. Unknown to us then of course, this was, in ancient Chinese custom, an expression of its owner's wealth.

From the aforementioned, it is evident that violence was perpetrated against the community, but what about the violence that was supposed to exist within its confines? In 1989, Associated British Ports, celebrating the 150th year of Cardiff Docks, published an article by an unidentified author entitled *Cardiff & Barry - a double celebration*. This article referred to the origins of the area's violent reputation, which began during the 19th century boom in commercial activity. It stated:

Cardiff docks experienced a spiraling crime rate. Violence, street fighting and general mayhem became common place in the dock area. The over worked city police were loath to extend their activities to dockland, and gradually the idea of starting a private force gained favour. In 1865, the Third Marquess of Bute was given authority to start recruitment and shortly afterwards the Bute Docks Police Force came into being. Their impressive motto was 'Wrth Ddwr a Thân' - By Water and Fire. [This motto was in fact used much earlier by the Taff Vale Railway Company. Author.]

Within a few months it was clear that the new force was a success. Dockland crime was reduced to manageable proportions and rioting was almost non-existent. Such a dramatic fall in the crime rate was hardly surprising as the dock police would be armed with sabres as they set off to restore law and order.

Although the commercial activity would diminish, the reputation of the allegedly violent nature of our community would last to the current day. In addition to violence, gambling in the streets was also among the many vices of the day which the police were expected to prevent. As it was illegal — unlike the gambling fever inspired by the National Lottery of today — this unlicensed activity also contributed to Tiger Bay's unsavoury reputation. During my childhood days in the 1950s, there was only one gambling corner going strong. This was located outside The Marchioness of Bute pub on the corner of Sophia and Angelina streets. In 1967 W Wabelus, an old Docks Boy, then resident in Llanrumney, outraged by a version of life in Cardiff's Tiger Bay as described in Stan Hugill's *Sailortown* (a then recently published book), wrote a letter on 18 August to the *South Wales Echo* entitled *Tiger Bay was never like this!* He stated that Hugill's interpretation was:

> … certainly not true of the docks district as I remember it from 1895 onwards.

> The examples of violence he quotes were the exception rather than the rule. Most people lived orderly lives.

I lived in the lower part of Bute Road from 1895 until 1899. I can remember standing in the doorway of the bank behind St. Stephen's Church watching through the open doorway a clerk weighing out golden sovereigns to customers.

Would that be possible in the sort of society Mr. Hugill describes? It is true that in Bute Road shops of all kinds of weapons were openly for sale. There were daggers, revolvers, knuckle dusters, etc. Yet I do not think there were as many cases of stabbing as there are today. Of course, owing to the cosmopolitan nature of the docks population there was bound to be some trouble.

Bute Road had a smell of its own from the cooking that came from the seamen's boarding houses. Every one of these had to be licensed.

I have walked through Tiger Bay and Bute Road for over 70 years and have never been molested. ... It was not all degradation in the docks.

Things had clearly changed by the beginning of the twentieth century, as no one in the community recalls seeing sabre armed policemen patrolling the streets of Tiger Bay or the Docks. As the memory of its former boom town violent days held sway outside the community far longer than reality dictates, the chapters that follow will attempt to bring to fore the *real*

Many a seaman of Sailor-town found a temporary home before 1963 at the many boarding houses which stood on old Bute Street like the Chinese one shown above or the many others in the back streets throughout the community. (Photo courtesy of BHAC)

day-to-day existence of a community, admittedly not perfect, but far removed from such engaging myths of violence.

Setting aside issues of violence, real or mythological, for the moment, today's city of Cardiff takes pride in its reputation as being the port from which the *S.S. Terra Nova* set sail in 1910 on Captain Scott's expedition to discover the South Pole. But enthusiasm for the Terra Nova was also shared by seven year old Beatrice Dyer-Griffiths who spent her childhood days in Loudoun Square, living just two doors away from Dr Gervan's surgery in the heart of Tiger Bay.

"I must get Captain Evan's autograph," Beatrice thought to herself one day. One of her earliest memories was of "taking" her sister's autograph album to get the captain's signature. Hastily making her way to the east Dock through the Sophia Street entrance on Bute Street, she was totally enthralled at the sight of the *S.S. Terra Nova,* whose masts seemed to reach to the sky as the ship came into view. As she walked along the quayside she could see the gangplank ahead of her.

"What are you doing there!" said a booming voice that had the effect of turning her legs to jelly and bringing her down to earth by its authoritative command. She stopped dead in her tracks.

"I ... I ... I only want Captain Evans' autograph, Sssir," she said, fearing she was about to be arrested.

The S.S. Terra Nova sailing out of Cardiff Docks to the South Pole in 1910. (Photo courtesy of BHAC)

"Give me that book," said the awe inspiring figure standing before her. And she fearfully handed over the book.

"I died a thousand deaths," Beatrice recalls, "as my sister

had all Glamorgan Cricket names in it, as well as Cardiff Rugby Club."

"What if it was lost? I shouldn't have taken the blasted book, but I did. What shall I do if I don't get it back? How am I going to explain this to my sister?" These were the thoughts that roamed around her troubled mind. She needn't have worried, of course, as the book was brought back to her with the captain's signature and a verse which stated:

> Always eat when you feel hungry,
> Always drink when you feel dry,
> Always sleep when you feel sleepy,
> Don't stop breathing or you'll die.

Recalling that pleasant memory at the age of 95, Beatrice Griffiths looks back on a Tiger Bay childhood unmarred by the violence that legend would suggest. Of course, not all violence is physical, and once again, reports in the *Western Mail* place in context the attitudes widespread during those times. Frederick de Courcy Hamilton, who had played a major role in getting the Coal Exchange built in Mount Stuart Square, and Revd. John Thomas, were self-promoted arbiters of morals for the day. In a report of a Bible Society meeting in the 20 November 1917 edition, under the heading MORALS OF CARDIFF, Mr de Courcy Hamilton made some strong references to immorality in Cardiff. He wrote:

> that Cardiff girls were sold into white slavery every night -
> young girls in their teens. The Rev. John Thomas would bear
> him out...

On Saturday, December 29th, de Courcy Hamilton and his cohorts initiated the Victory Campaign which, according to the *Western Mail* (31.12.1917), identified:

> … that slums and disorderly houses flourish in the heart of the
> city; that there is a great increase in the alien population, many
> of whom are able to buy property at fancy prices and clear out
> British residents; that young girls come from all parts as
> servants to lodging-houses and in a short time cohabit with the
> aliens; that there is shameless loitering of women; … that
> strenuous efforts are being made to set up in other parts of the
> city pitfalls recently removed from off Bute Street, Wood
> Street and St Mary-street…

As the latter streets mentioned in the report are, of course, in the
centre of Cardiff, not in Tiger Bay at all, it is reassuring to know
that vice at that time was found throughout the city and not just
in Tiger Bay. But even though de Courcy Hamilton recognises
that:

> [s]lums and brothels flourish in the heart of the city

his concern is with the:

> [g]reat increase in alien floating population. About 1,100
> Arabs, 600 or 700 coloured men from the desert, from East and
> West Africa, Chinese and other Asiatics, are earning high
> wages. Aliens are able to buy property for fancy prices and
> clear out British residents… (*Western Mail*, 14.1.1918).

By this time, its honorable secretary Rev. John Thomas who
had renamed the campaign the "Victory Crusade Movement,"
also feared that "Fully-licensed restaurants, with music and
dancing, are a grave menace to our young people to become
both intemperate and immoral." As already pointed out by
Rev. Thomas and de Courcy Hamilton, "Cardiff girls were sold
into white slavery every night - young girls in their teens."
Apparently WHITE WOMEN IN ALIEN BOARDING
HOUSES had also become a "Cardiff Problem." On 17 January
1918, the *Western Mail* had occasion to report under the
aforementioned headline:

The presence of white women in the boarding houses for alien seamen was discussed by Cardiff Health Committee on Wednesday, Alderman Dr. James Robinson presiding.

Chief-inspector Samuel Evans was asked if there were any white women in the seamen's boarding houses, and his reply was that there were some white women who worked in the houses during the day, but they did not sleep there at night-time.

The Chairman: You will see that no white women are employed in these houses, and if they are you will report to this committee when you bring forward the applications for licenses. We can refuse to grant the licenses if we find that white girls are employed.

Mr. William Grey: I see by the papers that they advertise for girls as servants.

Mr. G. F. Willett: The white girls rush down there…

After the latter had *rushed down there*, the days when men of the cloth had the audacity to come into the area and denounce white women who married non-white men as whores or prostitutes, even though properly wed in St Mary the Virgin Church or the Registry Office, were soon to come to an end. This form of blatant and unadulterated racism began to metamorphose into a more benign and subtle one. Particularly after de Courcy Hamilton was eventually forced to appear at the Swansea Assizes for slanderous remarks about women in the community made on 14 November 1917 at the World's Fair off Bute Street which were overheard by police constable Simms who was on special duty at the event.

It has to be said at this juncture that such fringe activities as took place in or near the industrial docks or in the backs of some dubious cafés were in stark contrast to the hard working families that formed the community at large. Bay people were broad-minded and tolerant enough to accept that there were ladies of the night and often turned a blind eye to them plying their trade aboard the ships in the docks. But should every mother and wife be tarred with the same occupational brush purely because of this tolerance? Sensible folk would think not, but even in 1993, decades after the decline of shipping, it was necessary to parry offensive descriptive remarks in the press. These suggested that by the 1980s Butetown "had become a hag-ridden haunt of prostitutes and drug dealers" — as was boldly stated in a late December issue of the *South Wales Echo*. "PROSTITUTES in Cardiff are about to swap the street life for the country life. They are going on a weekend of canoeing and rock-climbing," was the lead for a report in a national newspaper of the same year. Entitled *The Girls from Tiger Bay Take to the Hills*, Martin Wroe's article on the front page of *The Independent*, 4 May 1993, entertainingly went on to report that:

> 12 members of the city's flourishing community of prostitutes will exchange stilettos for sensible walking shoes, wave goodbye to the red lights and set off in a minibus for the Brecon Beacons.

I hope the *flourishing community of prostitutes* of so many other British cities get the opportunity for a break. Clearly, in the case of Cardiff, both reports referred to activity around the Custom House pub, near the centre of town, the last bastion of such pastimes which was recently demolished to make way for the new Bute Square. Standing as an oasis on the derelict land that once was Crichton Street and former home to the Greek and Cypriot community, this area has long been isolated from the remaining community. Incidentally, the final paragraph of a rebuttal that I wrote to the first article, published by the *South Wales Echo* on 27 December 1993, indicated:

> Our community is under constant observation and study by various academic groups and other authorities and your offices are only a hop, skip and jump from our community for you to

With regard to drug dealing, the use of cannabis among a certain sophisticated element in the community is ancient and can hardly warrant the term *drug dealers*. However, since that rebuttal, concern has been growing in the community at the increasing use of crack cocaine which has insinuated itself among the young.

Prostitution and drug dealing remain potent weapons in the arsenal of the press for its misrepresentation of Tiger Bay. In the past the media also demonstrated its prowess in the subtle reproduction of racism when it reported the trial of twenty-eight year old Somali seaman Mahmood Mattan, who retains the ignoble reputation of being the last man to be hanged in Cardiff.

Although he was a seaman who stayed in the boarding houses of Tiger Bay, his family, which included three sons at the time, were raised outside of the area on David Street. Omar Mattan, one of his sons, said the reemergence of his father's case in Chapter Six of *The Tiger Bay Story* encouraged the relaunch of a campaign for his father's exoneration. Subsequent to its publication in 1993, the BBC made a documentary about the family's plight, positioning the matter once again in the headlines.

However, headlines have been used by the press in the production of racism and the example from the *South Wales Echo and Express* of 24 July 1952 which follows is indicative of this subtle linguistic strategy.

SOMALI 'A SEMI-CIVILISED SAVAGE' 'Tried To Lie His Way Out' is a characteristic example of the reporting style employed by journalists that demonstrates the strategic reproduction of racism. For example, hidden within this headline, which alleges to summarize the lead story of the report on page three concerning Mahmood Mattan, who stood accused of the tragic murder of Butetown shopkeeper Lily Volpert, is the deliberate intention to place Mattan in a negative position. This intention is deciphered through its ability to bias the opinion and understanding of its readership and through its potential to influence the reader's interpretation of the text.

For example, the lead sentence in the text begins, "Counsel defending a Somali accused ...." As in the story of the *dangerous negro* mentioned earlier who ran amok in Cardiff, it appears

Mahmood Mattan (centre right) with Somali friends in the back room of Berlin's Milk Bar on Sophia Street. Circa January 1950.
(Photo courtesy of Hulton Getty)

that the journalist considered it important to identify Mahmood Mattan in terms of his nationality rather than by his name, or even with the term "man." Also in the paragraph is the expression "this half-child semi civilised savage" which demonstrates a similar function to the headline. That is to negatively characterise Mahmood Mattan before the reader has interpreted the rest of the story. Furthermore, the headline has the power to influence the reader by making an associative link with other members of the Somali community thereby placing them also in a negative light.

Because the headline is a grammatically incomplete sentence, its lack of clarity also leads to a certain ambiguity as to why the defence counsel is condemning Mattan. Such device may also influence the reader to condemn Mattan before reading the whole report and thus believe that he is guilty.

It could be argued from the positioning of these topics in the headline that this is the most important information of the news report. Yet a close examination of the text reveals this is not the case. The most important information, not implied in the headline, is the fact that Mattan's defence counsel's argument stated that *a lot of the evidence against Mattan was circumstantial, and that he was relying upon the evidence of the prosecution witness alone to build Mattan's defence.* Without doubt, the defence counsel's inadequate defence resulted in Mattan's conviction. Moreover, it is devastatingly clear that the headline reflects the beliefs and attitude of the newspaper which possessed the power to influence public outrage against an innocent man.

Thus it happened that the tragedy of Lily Volpert's murder was further compounded by the state murder of Mahmood Mattan, a member of Tiger Bay's old Somali community — which will be examined more closely in Chapter Eight.

Long-time resident Mahmood Kalineh failed in 1969 in his attempt to get a pardon for his countryman from the then Home Secretary James Callaghan but the campaign was relaunched in 1994 after Mattan's widow Laura wrote 200 letters to MPs, councillors and community leaders in an attempt to enlist their help.

After the success of the publicity surrounding the case,

Cardiff solicitor Bernard de Maid offered his services to the family's cause and in 1998 the Court of Appeal told the family that Mahmood Mattan had in fact not committed the crime and would be given a posthumous pardon. However, as of this moment, the family still awaits compensation for its bitter years of suffering.[2]

Of course media representation of race was not always as subtle. For example, famous Welsh writer Howard Spring, once wrote that the children of Tiger Bay were the "fruit of frightful misalliances"! Fortunately I was blessed with a handsome father and a very beautiful and attractive mother as a result of such an alliance. And those historians who have claimed that the terraced back streets of Tiger Bay were lawless and only restored to order by the 1960s demolition are talking pure fantasy. To declare such a thing proves they have never walked those streets and enjoyed the companionship and camaraderie found in the old commu-

Gathering outside 19 Frances Street. In the background on the doorstep of No 18 is Noni Cameron and her sister Joan Dupree standing. In the foreground are (L to R) Anthony Evora, Terry Walli, Neil Sinclair and Leslie Sinclair-Clarke with daughters Vanessa and baby Melanie.
(Photo courtesy of the Sinclair family)

nity — or come to the miserable streets that have replaced them. For the record, Tiger Bay had the safest streets that any child could grow up on in Cardiff, as every adult took responsibility for their well-being.

Over the years the earlier blatant hostility began to

disguise itself. Nevertheless even in the 1950s "blackie" and the "N" word were still bandied about. But as I have previously said, times were changing and I have a strong memory while apprenticed to a printing firm in Cathays of being told that I lived in a slum. Not actually knowing what the word meant, it left me dumbfounded and embarrassed, as there was an obvious negative inference in its tone. When I got home that evening I looked at the outside of my home for the tell-tale signs, peeked into the immaculate parlour which was used only for visitors, into the living room and out into the back garden. For the life of me, I could not see the signs.

In time I began to hear that our houses were supposed to be smelly and dirty as well. But whose? Certainly not the Arabs from the Yemen who, for instance, kept spotless homes with white painted exteriors, some-times whole rows together, many of them with colourful Moorish tiles adorning their passages. Furthermore the proud mothers of the Bay cleaned inside and out constantly, sometimes to outdo one another. But the euphemisms for racism continued to rear up. Now the houses were over-crowded. Yet even this excuse is dubious, as thanks to the Marquis of Bute, there were many large houses in the area. Some, like Said Mohammed's in Peel Street, could house as many as 25 seamen and most of the huge houses were used for this purpose. My godmother Lillian Constance Reeves had two adjacent four-storey lodging houses on Patrick Street. Rather than being overcrowded, homes in the community were open house as folk enjoyed being around each other and simply loved to congregate.

This aspect of community life can be confirmed by outsiders, as many people from the valleys and the rest of Cardiff regularly made a beeline for the area because of its legendary friendliness.

"Nothing wrong with Bute Street!" I was told by an octogenarian resident of Llanharan, who in his youth played rugby at the Cardiff Arms Park. Turning down the barrel of beer and sandwiches laid on by the club after finishing a game, he and other rugby players would make straight for the Bay to celebrate and sing with the musicians and other revellers at the Cardiff International Athletic Club (the "CIACs"), or any of the then 93 still existing pubs in the locality. He especially liked the singing and music at Johnnie Erskine's Loudoun pub on Bute Street and the kiss on the cheek he always got from Auntie Ruby, Connie Ali née Shepherd's mother.

To its credit Tiger Bay, despite its mere one square mile geographical extension, has produced some of the country's most outstanding rugby players — among whom can be found Billy Boston, MBE, Johnnie Freeman, Colin Dixon, Gerald Cordle, Carl Smith, Danny Wilson and his football playing son Ryan Giggs, to name but a few. As his mother Yvonne Bishop was born and raised in Loudoun Square, Tiger Bay can also lay claim to the Ely-raised Steve Robinson who enjoyed tremendous success as a boxer during the mid 1990s until he lost his title to Sheffield's Prince Nazeem Hamed. In addition the area has produced several Shotokan Karate experts: Jeremiah "Jerry" Mbakwe and his younger brother Chuku, who are both Sixth Dan (Chuku is also world referee and judge of competition karate); Owen Sumner who is Fourth Dan; and Von Johnson.

Tiger Bay's own Billy Boston, MBE, in action, circa 1959.
(Photo courtesy of Helena Boston)

Given the incredible and disgraceful behaviour shown towards the residents of Tiger Bay by the media and some of the citizens of the host nation, one has to wonder who has the worst reputation, Tiger Bay or the City of Cardiff? I think it is high time that those historians and other detractors who wish to continue perpetuating Tiger Bay's bad reputation into the 21st Century examine their consciences, learn their history, recognise the subtle and disguised racism dormant there and cease and desist. Otherwise, to our nation's eternal shame, they will not only be denigrating Tiger Bay but exposing to the world one of the most torrid pages of meanness and spitefulness to be found in the annals of Welsh history.

As will be seen in the following chapter, one of the outcomes resulting from the host city's ostracism of and prejudice toward the Tiger Bay community has been its depiction of the area as a wild, jungle-like place at odds with civilization. A place in which the city was determined to keep the Tiger caged, as it would confine its wild animal namesake, in a zoo.

Chapter Three

NATURAL BARRIERS

Given the enduring omnipresence of *That Reputation*, one may wonder why Tiger Bay has remained so special to its inhabitants? Assuming it is not dysfunctional, it goes without saying, *There's No Place Like Home* and first and foremost Tiger Bay has been just that, a home. One however with certain unique qualities. If you think of the traditional idea of a village or working class community, where everyone lives as an extended family and knows everyone else intimately, then Tiger Bay was very much like this, with one major difference: its descendants hailed from native soil and from the seven seas, comprising more than fifty-seven different nationalities. Yet

Marcia Brahim-Barry, left, and cousin Angela at the front door of the Brahim family home at 30 Dudley Street, "down the docks!" Circa 1948.
(Photo courtesy of Marcia Barry)

they regarded themselves as one non-Balkanized community. Not only were there differing nations settling down together, but families that mixed religions, like the Brahim family down the docks end which had a Malay Muslim father and a Welsh Catholic mother. Situations like this often meant Christian food served while Dad was away at sea but halal meals cooked from diferring pots and pans when his ship came home.

Undoubtedly, circumstances such as these helped to solidify the foundation of the community's uniqueness.

Nevertheless, geographic location and architectural design also contributed to this cohesion. "Butetown has never been a ghetto like Harlem," said George Yeoman in *Butetown's role after Buchanan*, which appeared in an August 1968 *Western Mail*. "It can be argued that Cardiff's harmony stems from barriers between district and city … a segregation," he continued, "imposed by railways, industry and water, making conscious segregation unnecessary." As the community was an island unto itself, a narrow peninsula congested between the Clarence Road Railway and Glamorganshire Canal to the west, the Taff Vale Railway to the east, the Great Western Railway to the north and the sea to the south, more than likely these man-made and natural barriers are the basis for the aforesaid unity. Also, the Second Marquis of Bute, having the foresight to build

A 1950s view of the original Loudoun Square fondly remembered by residents of a certain age as it was before the tower blocks were built in the 1960s. (Photo courtesy of Olwen Watkins)

four parks or squares within the layout of the community, provided open spaces for residents to congregate, which further contributed to its closeness.

Historically the community of Tiger Bay and the Docks has always made strangers welcome. Although an extremely small one square mile area, which never exceeded 9,000 residents even at the height of its fame, or to some infamy, it nevertheless gained an international reputation.

This close-knit community, which existed since before the turn of the 20th century, was strengthened by the anti-Chinese riots of 1911 and the anti-Black race riots of 1919, mentioned in the previous chapter. Throughout and beyond the Edwardian era, it was accepted that non-European residents lived *in* Tiger Bay, but not that they should prosper and move out into other parts of the city. As I wrote in *The Tiger Bay Story*, as that century progressed, Tiger Bay became a safe haven from external violence. So while racial unrest occurred in London's West 11 during the 1950s, and in Liverpool 8 during the Toxteth disturbances of the Thatcher era, life in Tiger Bay and the Docks remained relatively immune to these social disturbances due to its "natural" barriers.

Thus, being hemmed in by the Glamorganshire Canal and the Great Western and Taff Vale railways helped to produce the multi-ethnic harmony I described in *The Tiger Bay Story*. However, a contributing factor, not mentioned in the latter was the life of seamen aboard ship. As the Merchant Navy ships that docked in Cardiff were predominantly manned by multi-ethnic crews, those who made Tiger Bay their home once ashore remained mates in the community, considerably diminishing ethnic conflict and difference.

History books do detail, for example, heated exchanges between Turkish and Russian ships which were kept at arms length, so to speak, in the port. But stories of life in the streets of a community less affected by such geopolitical conflict is what this book aspires to document. Thus, in what follows will be found a taste of the broth that was brewed in Tiger Bay's multicultural cauldron — like the incident that occurred — for example, on Nelson Street one day back in the 1920s…

"You black bastard!" snarled the young patrolling

policeman as he strode down the street past an approaching West Indian. Whether it was the insult or the officer's abuse of authority has not been easy to ascertain, but before the cocky officer had time to enjoy his momentary sense of power the victim of that slanderous remark spun around and grabbed him.

Of that maligned West Indian, Lord Callaghan once said, "there was one not mentioned in [*The Tiger Bay Story*], who, I recall, played quite a prominent part in Butetown forty years ago, in conjunction with Alan Shepherd. I refer to Jim Nurse, who was not a communist [like Shepherd], but who took a very strong position on issues like discrimination and racial prejudice. He was a very nice person and I remember him with affection."

Clearly Jim Nurse's passions had earlier stalwart beginnings, as in the ensuing battle that followed on Nelson Street, both men fell to the pavement, much to the surprise of other passersby. On the ground the officer struggled to grasp his truncheon, but Jim held his hand firmly on the officer's trousers preventing him from getting the weapon out. However, the offensive bobby got his whistle to his mouth. But before he could blow it, Danny Sinclair dashed out from among the crowd now gathered and, much to the amusement of the onlookers, pulled the whistle from the officer's mouth "false teeth an' all."

My grandfather Danny Sinclair who came to the aid of Jim Nurse in Nelson Street.
(Photo courtesy of the Sinclair family)

This was a later source of laughter for Danny and Jim, who had been gambling on a Maria Street corner not a few moments before the incident. Charlie Waith had been with them as well as two Arabs from Aden and Abdi Guri, a Somali seaman who arrived in the Bay at age seventeen and lived to the legendary age of 107. Retelling the story to their fellow gambling buddies would soon have its downside, as later that day Charlie saw a number of bobbies escorting Danny down to Canal Parade, a street of terraced houses that faced the old stone wall which separated the Glamorganshire Canal from the Tiger Bay community. There the police thrust Danny up against the stone wall, threatening him with their truncheons. However, when one of the policemen spied Charlie peeping around Nelson Street corner, they marched Danny off to Maria Street Police Station on the corner of Bute Street, where everybody knew, in the privacy of the cells, he'd get a good thrashing.

Danny Sinclair lived on the same street as his mate Charlie. In fact, in the early years of the twentieth century, Charles Beresford Waith was born in 28 Peel Street. His father, Mr Davis, was from the West Indies, but his mother came originally from Devonshire. Shortly after his birth, Doctor Gervin gave up hope for Charlie, so two matriarchs of the Bay, Auntie Seran and Auntie Edie Purvoe, took compassion on him — so they told him later in life — and he survived. But when he first attended South Church Street School he often fainted while standing and suffered many bilious attacks.

Charlie Waith was also one who witnessed the 1919 race riots referred to in *That Reputation* and *The Tiger Bay Story*.

"Don't go to work today, Bill," said Charlie's mother to his father, who worked in the chemical works near the docks. She was in dread of what might happen to her husband once confronted by the Irishmen of Newtown, who were lined up on the bridge at the top of Bute Street.

By this time, having arrived in the 1830s, "the Irish were integrated enough to be amongst the major assailants of blacks and Arabs in 1919, though perhaps this also shows the precariousness of the improved position of [their] community. An Arab and black invasion of 'their' quarter of the city threatened to place them back at the bottom of the pile,"[1] so Neil

Evans' account informs us of those turbulent days. In fact, the Irish who had established themselves in Newtown, a community on the fringes of Tiger Bay, were among the mobs who threw stones at people on Bute Street from the Taff Vale Railway embankment during the 1919 riots. Paradoxically, there were friendships between residents of Tiger Bay and Newtown, like that of my father Walter and his friends Bill and Gwilym Nichols, two brothers of Irish descent. Moreover, a number of black families resident in Newtown, like the parents of Robert Johnson, had even gained the respect of the Irish community predominant there.

Every day, as was his routine, Bill Davis used to go through Tyndall Street, the main street through Newtown, to get to his work.

"Yes! I'm going!" Bill said adamantly to his wife as he left his home and strode boldly up Bute Street intrepidly approaching the mob obstructing his path.

"Good morning, Bill," said the men as they opened the way to let this familiar figure of a man pass through with no trouble at all.

Charlie vividly recalled seeing a policeman hit over the head with a flagon of beer while his horse went through a bedroom window during the time the riots raged on. However, his more pleasant memories from those times recall the old women coming around with a basket, shouting "Fresh cockles, fresh cockles," and another who came with haddock in her basket, "Fresh haddock, fresh haddock." Or the man with

Tom the Fish, one of the more famous local street vendors, serving Esmay Sumner and her son Owen. Circa 1962.

(Photo courtesy of Jack Stevens)

a donkey and cart with all the black bananas in them that used to be quite sweet.

As already indicated, as a child Charlie Waith was a frail lad, who like so many until more modern times, left school at 14, yearning to follow in his father's footsteps and go to sea. Being of a rather delicate nature, the officers who saw him when he went down to the ship refused to take him due to his puny appearance. Somewhat dismayed he went to stay with his auntie in Maesteg where he, like a number of men of colour, worked underground in the mines for a time. However, by the time he was seventeen his chance to prove himself a worthy seaman arrived when his friend Isaac "Manny" Phenis came looking for him and encouraged him to make a "Pier Head Jump" — that is, go to sea by any means necessary. Thereafter Charlie made two trips to sea, and after spending some of his time in Sheffield, made one more trip before coming home to Tiger Bay. Of course, life went on in his absence.

"When I finally came home, nobody knew who I was," said Charlie as he returned to the gambling corner of old Maria Street and the fascinating street life of his home community.

By the 1950s the corner of Sophia and Angelina Streets had become the most renowned open-air casino in the area. Maltese, Greeks, black "Portugee" (Portuguese), Adenese (as men from Yemen were called then), men from a variety of West Indian islands and disparate parts of Africa rolled their dice at the penny or shilling schools which were played on that very corner. "On any fair weather day," I recalled in *The Tiger Bay Story:*

> Manuela's chair was placed outside her house in Old Angelina Street at the corner of Sophia Street right opposite Kerrigan's Marchioness of Bute. On that corner, in those days, was found the largest congregation of people outside of Loudoun Square Park. There Manuela sat, dressed in a floor length black skirt with her black shawl wrapped around her shoulders, observing

the gamblers rolling the dice outside Kerrigans. Like so many
other ladies seated outside their houses, Manuela observed the
corner of Bute Street to see if Bobbies, making their rounds
from Maria Street Police Station … were coming. "Heads Up"
was the signal shouted if the Bobbies appeared and in all the
excitement money and dice disappeared…[2]

Incidentally, this was a way some fearless children could
make a shilling. After shouting the signal, kids could run into
the circle, pick up a few pennies and run away while the men
were caught off guard. I admit to being one of them. However
the men, believe it or not, took this in the spirit of fun.

In the decades prior to the Second World War, most men
congregated on old Maria Street and gambled near the Cardigan
Pub, opposite the home of St Lucian-born seaman James
Ernest. Some young lads worked as 'shoe blacks,' polishing
and shining the shoes of the many dandies found in Tiger Bay
in those days. These shoe blacks often sat outside the Arab
cafés and seamen's boarding houses — like Hassan Malayo's,
where Malayan seamen tended to stay.

The largest crowds to gather in the streets of Tiger Bay,
however, were those that came out to show their respect for the
recently departed, resulting sometimes in magnificent funeral
processions.

In an undated letter to author Jeffrey Green, Donald
John, a one time resident of Loudoun Square, gave an interesting
description of the typical funeral processions that took place in
Tiger Bay at the turn of the twentieth-century and of the man
who led them. Although Barbadian seaman Uncle Ned Bovell,
also of Loudoun Square, would continue the tradition, John
wrote of his predecessor, Mr Vincent:

> … who always took the lead in every Black funeral procession
> in Tiger Bay. These were quite spectacular affairs, and
> something to see. Vincent would be immaculate in black

topper and a morning coat, white gloves, spats, and looking quite spendid, as he headed a retinue of similarly dressed black men walking in front of the hearse, which in those days always had a black horse, sometimes two, with black plumes on their heads, and sometimes the funerals were not only those of Black departed, but of white people, late residents of Tiger Bay, perhaps the white wife of some West Indian or an African, sometimes a well known white resident, but such was the respect accorded to every resident that it made no difference, Tiger Bay being such a well knit society of all its inhabitants, Black or White, but always walking in front would be Mr Vincent. The cortege would start from the home of the deceased, walk through the Bay, into the town for a half mile walk in procession, when everybody would board the carriages for the cemetery about 3 miles distant. I attended some of these affairs, and was always surprised at the attention given by the onlookers of the town, once they saw all those blackmen walking through town, and all looking so well dressed, with Vincent leading, now wearing his famous topper. Men onlookers would doff their hats, caps, or whatever, and there always seemed to be a respectful silence. Sometimes these funerals would stop the traffic, with a policeman holding back the flow, at intersections, but in those days that would not be

Typical Tiger Bay funeral procession along early 20th century Bute Street. (Photo courtesy of Butetown History & Arts Centre)

much of a problem, as most traffic consisted of horse drawn carts, vans, etc.[3]

At such times of bereavement, it was the custom to adorn the windows of a house with black curtains but sadly that tradition, unlike the funeral processions, has gradually faded from community memory.

By the 1950s Donald's sister Gwennie was living on Bute Street near the green and black marbled Adelphi pub but she and Donald had once lived on the east side of Loudoun Square. Jeffrey Green's interesting snippet of Tiger Bay life indicates that their father:

> was a sailor from Barbuda who deliberately settled outside Bute Town and its Black and other visible minorities. Married to a Welsh women, by 1911 Elvin John was living in Grangetown working as a labourer. His son recalled, as a small boy, seeing the huge carthorses being led into the building where his father worked. He went to sea on fishing boats, providing another memorable childhood recollection when he came home with a huge cod over his shoulder. At the time of his death in 1924 Elvin John was working in Cardiff docks.

> It was at that time that Donald John first made his way to Bute Town where, as he recalled in 1988, there were 'all those black faces and nobody saying "Nigger!"' Apart from his own brothers and sisters, there were only two or three other Black families in Cardiff outside Bute Town.[4]

In all probability, Joseph Friday and my maternal grandfather, who also resided in Grangetown, may well have been the very people he was referring to as living outside the natural barriers that defined Tiger Bay.

The Bute Street where Gwennie John once lived ran parallel with the Taff Vale Railway embankment which formed the community's eastern boundary. Beyond this border lay

Collingdon Road with its many factories, granary warehouses and dockland businesses. Today, of course, the regeneration program has completely transformed the latter road into a avenue designed to be the new link between city and sea. Originally called Bute Avenue, it became Lloyd George Avenue when it opened in the year 2000.

"Bute Avenue should become Cardiff's place to see and be seen," said the title of the *South Wales Echo* Soap Box comment in the 5th October 2000 edition. It "has many benefits for visitors and people who live in the city," enthused one of Cardiff's youthful contributors in an account which continues:

> At last, we have a scenic route into Cardiff Bay! With all the fantastic developments that have gone on in the Bay over the past few years, making it a great place to go for a stroll at weekends, not to mention the fabulous restaurants, bars and other attractions that have opened there during recent months, it is about time the city had a pleasant way of getting to them on foot.

Clearly too young to recall the intriguing character of old Bute Street but not so young to be persuaded to stay away, this enthusiastic citizen of Cardiff seems to be unaware that, parallel to Lloyd George Avenue, Bute Street, which once included the Hayes on its route to the sea, travels alongside a community whose access to both city centre and sea is the best in Cardiff on foot or otherwise. The article continues:

> It's a shame the new waterfront has been virtually cut off from the city centre since its development. And, not having a car, it has been very difficult for me, and for many people I know, to get to the Bay.

Since *That Reputation* obviously still has the power to dissuade some of Cardiff's youth from strolling down Bute

Street, for those without means of transportation the Taff Vale Railway has provided, for more than a century and a half, a *safe* alternative means to arrive at the seafront.

Notwithstanding this, the exuberance of the youthful contributor does express the delight of the city's residents that:

> we now have what is to become a scenic route to the Bay's new attractions, making it easier and more pleasant to travel from the city centre for a day out.
>
> I've heard this new Bute Avenue has been called the 'Welsh Champs Elysees'.
>
> Having visited Paris a few times and being a real fan of the French capital, it would be great if the Welsh capital could transform this tree-lined avenue, into a popular place to meet friends and stroll along when the weather is fine – like the French original.
>
> It is also good to hear that jobs could be created for thousands of people through the new project to transform the city.
>
> Cardiff is one of the fastest growing cities in Europe and, in order to attract people from all over Wales and the rest of the world, we have to make every part of the city attractive to them. And with this new road, along with the National Assembly and the range of high quality housing which is springing up in the Bay, this part of Cardiff is just another reason we should be proud of the city.

One thing that can be said for the residents of Tiger Bay is that they were *always* proud of their community. However, after living on a building site since its 1960s demolition and suffering twelve years of "regeneration" for the creation of a waterfront development that *has been virtually cut off from the city centre*, few local people have benefited in the slightest from the promise of new jobs. An examination of the price local residents have paid for this new development of which Cardiff can be so proud, is not without merit.

In 1993 South Glamorgan councillor Ben Foday, a native of Sierra Leone who represented Butetown at the time, made a demand "for unemployed people in a deprived area of Cardiff to be given first choice of construction jobs on the Cardiff Bay barrage." His appeal was made after a county council report revealed unemployment in the area to be 28.7 percent. He told the *South Wales Echo* of 16th November 1993, "I am also very concerned that Cardiff Bay's relocation programme means that many firms in Butetown have had to move to other areas" … increasing … "travelling costs for people in the area, many of whom are on relatively low wages."

In 1996, after the birth of the Unitary Authority to which councillor Foday was appointed by Welsh Secretary William Hague, he was still campaigning to "help the Cardiff Bay Development Corporation beat unemployment in the Bay." Unemployment statistics for that year showed 50% for the 20-30 age group in Butetown prompting him to say on, 5th April 1996: "The unemployment level(s) in Butetown is unacceptable."

Of course at the bottom of the avenue is the Cynulliad Cenedlaethol Cymru and it was the new Welsh National Assembly that published the *Multiple Deprivation 2000 Report* that described Butetown as "the most deprived ward in Cardiff." The fact that these circumstances have not improved as yet is undoubtedly a contributing factor to the current despondency in the community.

Looking back on more prosperous times, it must be asked what was so unpleasant or unattractive about old Bute Street? Only old photographs can now remind us of the grand architecture many of the street's buildings once exhibited, only the original part of Bute Street, near what is now Mermaid Quay — the one part that the Marquis of Bute would still recognise — can remind us of its previous grandeur. But even there, in the autumn of 2000, the mahogany doors of one of Cardiff's grandest banks were closed as the bank relocated to smaller premises. As we enter the modern banking world of single teller and do-it-yourself banking, local residents will no longer experience the sense of majesty the old Westminster Bank building of both West Bute and Bute street has provided since the heady days of the economic boom of the 1920s.

A touch of grandeur once found on Bute Street remains captured in this photo-graph of the John Cory Sailors' and Soldiers' Rest which stood where the modern shops near Loudoun Square stand today.
(Photo courtesy of Idris Bowen FRPS)

But what does an old Bay Boy *good and true* have to say about the street he lived on during its interesting heyday? Ken Marshall, who came from Woolwich, south east London before residing at 214 Bute in 1937, took us for a stroll along his street after submitting a letter to *The Voice Of The Tiger*:

I stayed with my aunt Mrs Anne Saleh (nee Sullivan) and my grandfather as you passed over the canal bridge. Next to the *Bridge Hotel* was the Salvation Army Hostel then Saint Mary's infant, junior and girls' school. On the corner of South Church Street stood the renowned *Rothesay Castle Hotel*, known to one and all as the *House of Blazes*, next door but one or two was the *Bute Tavern*, sometimes referred to as The Green House, whose landlord was Mr E Radmilovic the renowned Welsh swimming champion. He was a very powerfully built man and an exceptionally strong person who could take on (may it be needed!) two men at the same time with ease and put them both out of action! A little further down, before the Police Station at Maria Street, was a boarding house owned by Mrs Joe Mercia, his wife and daughter, Ruby Mercia.

Opposite the Police Station was a Chemist shop and Richie "Knocker" Davies lived above with his mother. Then started the Financial Centre of the Bay. *Zussons* pawnshop was a place where a good suit, jewelry or a Japanese tea or coffee set would pay the rent and put food on the table until the seaman's ship sailed home from a voyage and was paid off. Then there was *Mr & Mrs Omar's General Store*. Their son was Gandi Omar. Next were two Arab boarding houses and the Norwegian Seaman's Hostel. Also an Arab *Zouwia* or school two evenings a week for any nationality who wished to learn the Arabic language and the basic Islamic greeting and farewell: "As Salaam Aliccom." Next came five flats where my aunt occupied the bottom floor.

Mr & Mrs Charlie Marshall (no relation) who later ran a bake shop at the bottom of Maria Street and Canal Parade and had two children, Howard and Musha [lived nearby]. Also Mr & Mrs Lappit with two sons Norman and Ronald. Next came the *Candle King Store* managed by Charlie & John Tubsell from Hunter Street, Docks. Then there was Mrs Morgan the Draper's shop before *Owens Chemist Shop* replaced it. Fortunately my aunt and Mrs Lappit moved to South Church Street and the Marshals to Canal Parade before the centre of this block of premises was destroyed by a parachute mine in 1941-1942.

The corner of Sophia Street started with *Sam On Yen*, the only Chinese Restaurant in Cardiff at that time followed by Mrs Hutchins' *Faggot & Peas Shop* and Volperts *Seamen's Store* and *Cardigan House* where local character Alex the Jew lived. Known as the Condom King as he went around the community furtively purveying those at that time unmentionable products. Also Henry Corne's Tailor Shop next to the *John Cory Seaman's Mission* and Mr Harry Milton's Newsagent.

On the next corner was the *Freemason's Hotel* or more dramatically The Bucket of Blood, the *Adelphi Hotel* and Mr & Mrs Gamlin, aunt of Ken Miller of Loudoun Square (who used to carry the Boys Brigade's flag at the front of processions). Then the *Loudoun Hotel* where Joe Erskine's father Mr Johnnie Erskine was landlord. Further down the block was a care boarding house owned by Louis Fennech, the *Greyhound Café*, and the Williams' Newsagents. Shop assistant, Joan Smith of Frances Street, whom I have known since I was twelve years of age, was a lovely person and Docks girl. The Oram Brush Company on the corner of Patrick Street which employed several women and girls from the Docks area and later the *Colonial Centre* occupied a building on the next block before West Bute Street in 1943-44.

Ken's journey reminds us that at the Colonial Centre, "The American jive dancing era was very popular with the Docks Boys and Girls" — as *Entertainment Below The Bridge* will later elaborate. Nearby the Draper Shop that Ken mentioned, which preceded Owens Chemist on the corner of Sophia Street, lived the family of Billy Douglas who ran the antique shop that came about after the untimely death of Lilian Volpert. His sister Patti still remembers with affection Miss Boe, a Norwegian lady who lived near Mrs Morgan's Draper Shop in the Norwegian Seaman's Hostel, which was destroyed in 1941 by the parachute mine that Ken Marshall alluded to earlier. Often invited into their home, Patti remembers Miss Boe's mother making waffles on the huge old-fashioned stove in her kitchen.

"They always talk about Mrs Capener and what she did for the

Mrs. Darby, our very own Patti Douglas, with baby Ian in her arms and Dennis Hippolyte sitting on the steps of Nora Glasgow's 1940s Loudoun Square home. Nora's mother Blodwen, one of the few Welsh speakers left from earlier times, stands in the shadows of the front door. (Photo courtesy of Hulton Getty)

children down the Bay but no one seems to remember Miss Boe," Patti said at an after funeral party held in the Paddle Steamer in 1999, fondly recalling how Miss Boe was kind to local children and sewed dresses for many of the less fortunate girls who needed them to go on community outings to the country.

The architecturally impressive *John Cory Seaman's Mission* that Ken Marshall also referred to has now been replaced by the Bute Street shopping centre, a series of ugly buildings which contain the only shops that service a community which once had shops on every street corner. But even these few remaining shops have felt the impact of the closure of businesses on Collingdon Road which has been replaced by the new Lloyd George Avenue. Among the casualties of progress, these shops, which perform an invaluable role in the community, are the Halal Butcher, Nessar Ahmad's grocery shop and the Fish & Chip Shop inside Loudoun Square, which without question has the best of such cuisine in the area. Raymond Abdul Rahman, its Pakistani owner, who arrived in Tiger Bay before the demolition, has seen his trade plummet not because Harry Ramsdens has appeared on the seafront but as a result of the loss of business from the compulsory purchase closures along the aforementioned Collingdon Road and the loss of industry along Dumballs Road located on our western boundary. In those not too distant days, local families would not buy fish and chips at lunch time because of the long queues of workmen from the other side of the railway.

Initially, the plans for Lloyd George Avenue required the removal of the railway wall to link the old community with that of the new in Atlantic Wharf. Any resemblance to the Berlin Wall is purely coincidental as the Iron Curtain only arose and fell during the twentieth century while the wall on Bute Street supporting the Taff Vale Railway has been standing since 1842. Its demolition was dependent upon the building of a new rapid transit rail link intended to run from the city centre down to Mermaid Quay. However, as no tramway has been included in the building of the avenue, the railway embankment and its grey stone wall will remain, as Railtrack is in the business of laying track and not tearing it up. The Bute Street wall captured the attention of architect David Mackie, a member of the design team for the Avenue from Barcelona, who was very impressed with its stone work and wondered why anyone would want to pull it down. This view is shared by many Bay folk.

Encapsulating this sentiment, Danny, a fictional character loosely based on my father's father, turns to the audience in the last act of *Tiger Bay Moonshadows* and says:

> … And now there is talk that the wall on Bute Street is going to come down. I have always felt that wall as a kind of security — a … wall of protection. Protecting a cosy community, an urban village, nested in a sprawling city… If the wall does come down it will be like our heart is being exposed — like a severe wound in our soul. Let's hope it won't be a mortal blow. I wonder sometimes will all the blood run out…

The tradition of grand funeral processions mentioned earlier continues to this day as the massive gathering for Victor Parker attested to in the early 1970s. But funerals were not the only processions in the community. Carnivals have also brightened the streets of Tiger Bay every August Bank Holiday weekend dating back to the early mid 1960s, a decade which also saw the beginnings of the Notting Hill Carnival in London. These events were a continuation of the church fetes where everyone pitched in to make them a success. In time they began to expand especially after Mrs Capener of *Rainbow Club* fame turned them into exciting social events. Growing in size with each year, a management committee became an essential element in their organisation and this committee, in turn, evolved into *Tiger Bay Community Arts*. By the mid 1990s some of the tireless members of this group included Keith Murrell, his sister Sheila Anderson and the indefatigable Humie Webbe, who is also the driving force behind Butetown's all female choir, *The United Harmony Singers* and the *Butetown School's Choir*.

One of the Deniz brothers playing his accordion at a local venue during the early 1950s.
(Photo courtesy of the Sinclair family)

In addition to the fascinating street life of the community, inside its confines could be found musical entertainers like

The Harlem Pages who toured Britain during the 1930s with Steffani's Silver Songsters. Rear left to right: Lawrence Denis, John Actie, Argie Finn Ishmael & Ahmed Farrah. Front left to right: Danny James, Arthur Young, Tommy Sinclair, Jocelyn Young & Sammy John.
(Photo courtesy of Julia Young)

guitarists George Glossop and the already mentioned Victor Parker (both of whom appeared in *The Tiger Bay Story)* and trumpet playing Cedric Ward. Obviously, there were many other entertainers —like the accordion playing Deniz Brothers of old Christina Street and Seffani's *Silver Songsters,* a group which made successful tours of Britain in the 1930s and included Nicky Dennis, Illtyd Lovelock, and Ross Johnson among others. A sub-group of the *Silver Songsters* was the all-black *Harlem Pages,* which included the likes of local Bay Boys Arthur and Jocelyn Young, Tommy Sinclair and Sophia Street's Sammy John among their ranks.

Having examined some of the events confined within the natural barriers of the streets of yesterday, our attention will now focus on some of the places where locals found and made their entertainment.

Chapter Four

ENTERTAINMENT BELOW THE BRIDGE

The Atlantic Wharf Leisure Village is an historical milestone. Among its entertainments, the UCI — that twelve screen multiplex cinema, which replaces the once derelict land of the West Bute Dock where no community previously existed — is the first official cinema ever to be built below the bridge. The only other establishment to function as a cinema, and that for one evening a week only, was the Wesleyan church in Loudoun Square, which will be discussed in the next chapter. Nonetheless, despite the recent development of the Leisure Village, it will take some time before locals regard the new entertainment complex as part of the traditional community of Tiger Bay and the Docks, even though it is only a stone's throw away.

In the minds of locals, the paucity of venues for local entertainment within the confines of the original community boundary today unmistakably contrasts with the number of places of entertainment available in the old community. Although I could only name forty-three pubs myself, this one square mile locality once boasted more than that, as history books speak of 140 in earlier times. However, public houses were not the only places where people congregated. One such place, remembered fondly by Charlie Waith, was the Angelina Street Mission.

"I used to go to the Mission and Whitsun Treats and one time in the Mission they had a magic lantern. We thought it was blinking marvelous, you know, to have pictures coming onto the screen — we really enjoyed that kind of thing," said Charlie in his own inimitable way.

"They talk about the good old days. Well when we was kids, it was good old days. There's no doubt about it compared with today anyhow," Charlie continues his reminiscences.

"On a Sunday we used to have to dress up in all our best clothes and go to see our grannies and that was like a religion!" And true enough this was a tradition shared by many other families that lasted right up to the demolition.

Typical Tiger Bay gathering outside the Angelina Street Mission during the 1920s. (Photo courtesy of BHAC)

Besides prayer meetings and Sunday School, the Mission also served as a concert hall. Among the talent to appear there during the late 1920s and early 1930s was Etta Purvoe — who was also the community midwife — Anna Emtage, Sarah Jane Waith, Kittie Campion and a few more not mentioned by Charlie. He was especially impressed by the vocal performances of Billy Purvoe: Billy sang a couple of songs "and it was quite interesting to hear him sing. But I don't know what you'd think of him today," said Charlie, who at the age of 81 still had a good memory and voice to give us his rendition of *Hezekiah Johnson's Jubilee* — a song which Billy used to sing and which was still heard in my youthful days in Tiger Bay:

Hezekiah Johnson so it appears,
Well he hadn't been a born just gone 50 years;
When he sat up to writing to his friends to say,
Boy we're all going to have a Jubilation Day;
Well black and white boy they came at night,
There they sat now and didn't they go,
They were a puffing and a blowing like a blacksmiths bong;
But some of those coons boy they never used spoons;
They might have used a spoon at the Mission Tree,
But they all used shovels at the Jubilee;
But first the parson now he gave up thanks,
Then they brought in soup in great big tanks;
When he saw the soup they began to grin,
And the ladies and the gentlemen they all dived in;
They swam around and some got drowned,
They snucked up all that meat inside;
Poor Sammy had the year to raw that night,
But still they swam and the Parson Sam;
He offered up a prayer for those are diseased,
With a mouth full of puddin' at the Jubilee;
Then Suzie Smart she dropped her tart,
She said oh help a me find this Sam,
There a couple o' my gold teeth in a jam;
We had a city cake it was nice hard bake,
We had a rice cake plum cake energy,
We had a stomach ache too at the Jubilee;
Then Hezekiah Mike rope 6 foot 10,
He walked right into the room and then,
Whose been a kissing my wife says he,
And every blinking nigger all around Not me;
Then razors flew and bottles too;
One poor cooly hollered Holy Mose,
Has anybody round here seen my nose;
Then Martin Smith boy he has a biff,
And on his grave was a RIP,
But he died like a hero at the Jubilee;
Then they all shook hands and said goodbye,
As happy as they could be because they all aloud
They had the time of their life at Johnson's Jubilee.

Although time has brought about imperfections to the
original lyric of *Johnson's Jubilee*, it is important to keep a

remembrance of its vitality. Obviously meant for amusement, some of the words in its lyric would offend the politically-correct ears of nowadays. Nevertheless, it is a song of its time. Moreover, there are not many today who know the complete song. Tommy Sinclair was one who kept the tradition of singing *Hezekiah Johnson's Jubilee* alive at many a Cardiff International Athletic's Club gathering when the club premises still existed at the town end of Bute Street. But Billy Purvoe had other songs in his repertoire, like the titleless one that follows:

Loudly the bell in the church started ring
Here's to my pa Jimmy Brown I did sing
Jimmy take care don't go in there
Danger is near so beware, beware, beware;
Take my advice but I've been there twice
so beware, beware;
When Jimmy had been married a month or so,
He quickly found out he'd been sold;
His wife she could drink like a blummin' fish,
Which barely sent Jim up the pole;
When he came home from work one day,
Down on the sofa as usual she lay;
He said in dismay well I declare and,
He dragged her off by the mop of her hair;
He said I don't love in September as I did in May,
And he hit her in a good old fashion way;
But Jim's wife seized a gallon jug,
And she almost smashed his mug,
And he wen' unconscious from September until yesterday.
Now Jim's wife she sent for her dear Mama,
Too upset about poor Jim;
Jim heard Ma telling the wife one night,
That she'd make it up for him so one night,
When it was nice and dark,
Jimmy arose like a blummin' lark;
He went away to Spain to stay,
He left a note to his Ma-in-law to say:
Goodbye my Ma-in-Law I've had enough of your jaw,
I'd like to choke you, you bald headed old cat,
But then if some day I'll come back to thee,

That'll be in the cemetery;
Goodbye my Ma-in-Law goodbye.

There were natural-born and trained musicians scattered about the old community. My mother often spoke of her childhood friend Lilian Jemmott, who played the piano marvelously. Lilly's West Indian father had a café on Bute Street — on the bridge opposite what eventually became the Rainbow Club — where he raised his musically talented daughter. While Lilly and Beatrice were still teenage girls, Lilly met up with a handsome African man whom she married. My mother attended their wedding, shortly after which they went away to Africa, a place Lilly had romanticised. Understandably she was surprised to find, having transported her electric sewing machine to her new homeland, that no electricity was available there in those days. But even more of a culture shock awaited her at the realisation of the polygamous environment she had married into. Approximately forty years later, during the late 1960s, Lilly eventually returned home to her beloved Tiger Bay community, which by then had been transformed into the Butetown council estate. Once resettled in Nelson House, one of the Loudoun Square tower blocks, my mother became reacquainted with her childhood friend until Lilly finally died a few years later.

Thus it was much to my surprise when I came across a paragraph in the *Black Edwardians*, a book I happened upon while browsing in the Central Library in Cardiff, that "Another Black worker who settled in Cardiff after time at sea was John Benjamin Jemmott, who was a merchant navy fireman aged twenty-seven when he married Alice Jones in 1908. Their daughter Lilian Louise Jemmott was born at 15 Bute Terrace on 6 January 1909. Street directories reveal that this was a boarding house and refreshment rooms for the Jemmotts until 1911, when they moved their dining rooms to 49 Bute Street, where they remained until 1927... This was not a poverty striken family: Lilian had piano lessons, passed college examinations, and married a doctor from Nigeria."[1]

For a place like Tiger Bay the 10 o'clock closing of pubs, dictated by the licensing law of the day, was far too early. As a result, just as an evening was about to get going, many a home was transformed into a shebeen, a private house where locals flocked to buy after-hours drinks and have a good night out after paying to enter. Henry Bassey ran one such place on Bute Street, us-

A 1970s view of No 52 at the top of the bridge on old Bute Street just prior to its demolition. My mother's friend Lilian Jemmott once lived at No 49 in the 1920s. The steps below the bollards at the right led down to the West Junction Canal mentioned in Chapter Seven. (Photo courtesy of John Briggs)

ing white chalk powder on the floors to make them slippery for dancing, as did Eva Dorning who eventually opened *La Estrella* down the Docks on Stuart Street.

Known for its exciting nightlife, many from the rest of Cardiff were also drawn to old Tiger Bay, despite its out-of-bounds reputation, for the best night out in town. Given *that reputation,* many of these visits by outsiders were often kept secret but the community's magnetic attraction overwhelmingly drew them to its many popular venues. One of the exciting haunts of those times which attracted many a good-timer was the *Big Apple.* During the mid 1940s for example, pianist Anthony 'Tony' Carter from Roath was a jazz enthusiast who often made a bee line for the club. He and other friends of his ventured down the dark lane that led to the excitement of the *Big Apple.*

This was the era of Stephan Grapelli and Django Reinhardt but among the local notables of the day who had made a name on the London scene were Nat Gonella and his New Georgians and Harry Parry who played with the likes of George Shearing and was the first to have a jazz programme on the BBC during the war. According to Tony, though they weren't particularly *into* the theoretical side of the music as were his jazz student friends, once the girls heard the beat they were up on the dance floor. Perhaps it was Millie Grant, but he does not recall the name of the sepia chanteuse that regularly sang at the *Big Apple*.

As it was the place to go, even Hazel Langford and her friend Maureen Jemmett, who were under age at the time, made their way down the lane to the *Big Apple*. Once up the rickety stairs, after they paid their entrance fee and successfully passed the scrutiny of Mr French who sat in a cubicle near the door, they entered the barn-like dance room of the club which was usually packed on a Saturday night with "after pub closing time" revelers. Once inside they met up with dancers Sheila Hutchins, Winnie Roberts and Bay Boys Johnnie Bute and Terry Jemmett, who were already moving to the ragtime style jazz that was popular during the 1930s and 1940s.

Still talked about today, the *Big Apple* was located near to the Sophia Street entrance of Bute Lane, the only remnant of which is the cobblestones found behind the Butetown Health Centre in Loudoun Square. Further down this same lane from this night spot was the rear of the Chinese gambling room where *Pakapue*, a sort of Chinese version of bingo, was played. As only the Chinese could play the game at the table, Hilda Ombull used to send her daughter Maureen with her ticket to the Bute Street entrance to see if she had won. Walter French, the West African owner of the *Big Apple*, made sure that once down the lane, which ran parallel to old Bute Street, you would hear the liveliest music in town resounding from inside its walls. Everyone wanted to be there, but some were not permitted to cross its threshold.

"You're Walter Sinclair's daughter!" the man at the door said to Lesley, my sister.

"He told me not to let you in."

While others more fortunate danced the night away to the sound of the *Muscat Ramble*, Lesley turned away in dismay leaving the lane as the music faded away behind her as she made her way home to Frances Street.

Eventually its African owner had been forced to close the *Big Apple* because fire regulations required extensive work to be done to make the club safe. However, before abandoning those premises, Walter French transformed the place into a school where he taught tap dancing. Some of his promising pupils, like Beryl Freeman and Maureen Jammett, left Cardiff in 1947 to appear in the successful London show *Four and Twenty Blackbirds*, while others, like Marie Actie and Violet Jammett, became glamorous show girls appearing in a 1950 show called *Harlem Comes To Town*. Personal details of the entrepreneurial Mr French have been provided by Iorwerth John, a Quaker who lived in Tiger Bay

Leslie Sinclair, age 16, who was turned away from the Big Apple by Mr French at her father's request.
(Photo courtesy of the Sinclair family)

during the second World War period. According to John, Mr French, who led an African group in the community at the time, "was very much for the establishment. He and his wife always well dressed and respectable. I once invited him and his wife home for a meal with my parents, as I knew it would please him. He had a concern to improve the education of the children in the

Docks and I introduced him to a lecturer from Darlington Hall Training College who was evacuated to Cardiff and who used to do things with a group of children after they had their tea."

Long before Cyril Clark, the proprietor of the famous reggae palace the *Casablanca Club*, was referred to as the King of Clubs by the *South Wales Echo*, the same Walter French was also boss of *The Colonial Club* on Bute Street just to the south of Patrick Street. Almost opposite the Taff Vale Railway Station, this was a meeting place for colonial merchant seamen and was managed by a rather distinguished toff-type, light-skinned gentleman known as Mr Pensoe. This very tall man's posh exterior was augmented by his many uptown visits to play tennis — which, of course, was a game of the upper classes then. He had an assistant who lived on Canal Parade whose name has become overshadowed by *Black Beetle*, the nickname locals conferred on him on account of his extremely dark complexion.

Bay Girls Marie Actie of old Christina Street and Violet Jammett of West Close as they appeared in Harlem Comes To Town in 1950.
(Photo courtesy of Violet Franklin)

Many local people worked at the club including barmaids Lydia Blackman and Flori Hassan-Ceasar and Mr Benjamin from Evelyn Street was the West Indian cook. Being a welcoming place, African-American sailors often frequented it and introduced a lot of the latest jive music to the locals. They even taught some of the more agile girls some of the best jive moves. Learning from the experts, these Bay Girls often stirred up a lot of envy when they travelled afar to Barry dances where they would take centre stage.

"Oh, here come the Docks girls!" a mumble could be heard from female onlookers.

The basement of the *Colonial Centre* was used as a makeshift dance school where many pupils were taught. Among the best were the late Josie Farrah and Laura Savage, taught by agile Bay Boy Raymond Noman. Josie, who we shall meet again in *Another River Out Of Eden*, was considered *dance on legs*, if ever such a description was possible. In time a stand alone annexe was added to the centre which would eventually be known as Frenchie's.

Those too young to go to such places had to make do with sneaking a peek through the windows to see, to the amazement of all, Josie being thrown over Richard "Timbo" Taylor's shoulders in superb choreographic excellence.

In the late 1950s some Bristol dancers demonstrated the "latest craze" on a TV Rock & roll show popular in South Wales and the West. They danced to Chubby Checker's *Let's Twist Again*. Of course down the Bay we had been doing the Twist the entire previous year. The shock of seeing a complete cock-up of

Exceptional dancer Josie Farrah is seen here standing to the left of local singer Winnie Roberts.
(Photo courtesy of Vera Johnson)

how the dance should be performed caused me to write to the BBC saying in protest: "That's not the Twist!" After all, Bronx-born GI Earl Jones and his airforce buddies, who came to Tiger Bay every weekend they had off, taught us how to do the Chicago version which had been made popular by *Hank Ballard and the Midnighters. The Midnighters* were already famous locally for their "never played on the airways of Britain" records *Sexy Ways* and *Work With Me Annie* and were the original exponents and recorders of the *Twist* that Chubby Checker would later take to world wide fame. However the earlier version of the Twist was slightly less energetic than the one which later became popular.

To my surprise, in response to mine, a letter came from the BBC to Frances Street requesting that I get a group together and show viewers how to *really* do the Twist. So I got Clara "Mingo" Graham, Beryl Freeman and Peter Phillips — the same Pete who to this day continues the tradition of leading funeral processions dancing in front with an umbrella New Orleans style — to go with me to the BBC studios which were then located on Cathedral Road.

When we were directed to get up to dance, instead of *The Midnighters* or even Chubby Checker on came the lastest *commerical* record called *The Peppermint Twist*, which caused us to gyrate at twice the speed of the real dance we had been doing for the entire previous year. In any event, *we* showed the viewing public how to do the Twist as we had been doing it in Frenchie's Annexe for some time! At the Annexe on Bute Street, a little closer to the sea just outside Tiger Bay, a wide variety of popular music was played from West African Hi Life, Caribbean Calypso to Fats Domino and Elvis Presley. Although I was under age, the people at Frenchie's ranged from late teenage to local friends' grandparents — all grooving and dancing together. The older people jived and swung their hips as ably as the young. They didn't feel too old for the music of the day. That's because authenticity resided in the soul of the music. The Tiger Bay and Docks community was highly critical about its musical taste, so British remakes of Rhythm & Blues originals didn't quite cut it and were often referred to as "Douggie." One instinctively knew the word meant "Square." The Yanks strongly influenced the musical tastes of Bay folk in those days, as they did in the days of *The Colonial Club*. The many GIs from the various American Air Force bases throughout Britain always brought original music to the streets of Tiger Bay — music that was not released in Britain.

Frenchie's Annexe was down the Docks, but a little further up Bute Street, near to South Loudoun Place in Tiger Bay was the *Ghana Club*.

"I well remember Benno Johnson opening the Ghana Club, which I used to frequent," said Lord Callaghan referring to its West African owner in a letter he wrote to me when I was editor of the *Butetown History & Arts Centre* magazine *The Voice Of The Tiger*. Prior to the days when the *Ghana Club* opened in 1957, James Callaghan had been our local member of parliament and was a guest in many local people's homes as well as our places of entertainment.

"On many occasions I have sat in Flori Fernandez' sitting room behind her shop in Bute Street and well remember the time she took Phil Edwards into her family in the customary manner that so many people in the Docks and Tiger Bay did," he remarked in that same letter. The Phil Edwards in question went on to make his mark in the world of boxing in later years.

Not only were clubs, pubs and missions well represented in the old community but barber shops as well — like the one at the top of old Angelina Street run by Afro-Portuguese barber Mr Fernandez, husband of the Flori mentioned by Lord Callaghan. He served the whole community but in particular men whose "nappy" hair texture was unfamiliar to barbers outside the community at that time. Naturally Bay Boys and Girls had to be well groomed to make their entrance into the many places of entertainment in the district. For women with such hair there weren't many, if any, salons to cater to their needs. Thus many a backroom in a house was used to handle this situation. Olwen Blackman's upstairs back room in Loudoun Square was one such makeshift salon where local girls could get their *hair pressed*, as they said. Being a multicultural community. all hair types were catered for there, but for those with the African variety, hot iron combs were used to straighten out the "naps" so the hair could be coifed into the latest style. Of course many learned how to do it themselves, placing their hot combs on the gas stove at home or even in the fireplace. Even some of the Bay Boys who frequented the Blackman family home in Loudoun Square wanted to have their hair pressed but, although fashionable among the GIs, I don't recall seeing that happen.

While Olwen straightened hair upstairs, she also taught local boys how to jive in the downstairs middle room where her grandmother used to live. Among that light-footed crew could be found Peter "Pepsi" Finlayson, Brian Actie, the twins Nino and Eric Adbi and Michael Santos.

Bay Boy recording artist Arthur Ford of Patrick Street performing as Gene Latter at the Butetown Carnival in 1983.
(Photo courtesy of John Taylor)

"Play that record!" Michael Santos would say, frequently requesting a calypso he was crazy about at the time.

Another Bay Boy of the same generation, seldom recalled, is Arthur Ford, known in the music industry as Gene Latter, who made a number of successful records in the early 1960s including *Sign On The Dotted Line*, *Tiger Bay* and *Little Piece of Leather*. In his youth, he was captured in a photograph taken at a party given in honour of the African American singing group *The Platters* at the George Street home of Rohima Ali in the 1950s.[2]

One outside the Bay who had a hairdresser's on Millicent Street in the days when Lermons and Lewises shops still graced the Hayes Bridge Road was Iris Harris. In the late 1950s, all the Bay and Docks girls went there, as Iris was one of the few non-black people in Cardiff who knew what to do with nappy hair. Hair pressed and done, the girls came away in the height of fashion with blond streaks highlighting the coiffure. Eliza Bassey also frequented the salon and kept her daughter Shirley informed of what the Bay Girls were having done to their hair. Some may remember the minor scandal when Raymond's of Mayfair damaged Shirley's hair. She would have done better had she gone to Iris's — like her mother and Helen Sinclair or Agnes Iruwa Mbakwe and her sisters Elizabeth and Kate.

Shirley Bassey, after her first appearance at Cardiff's New Theatre in the 1950s, is presented with flowers and chocolates by Monica Johnson & Fatima Mohammed, two local girls from the Rainbow Club.
(Photo courtesy of BHAC)

With fame came distance from her childhood friends and the Bay Girls with whom Shirley went into show business — like Lulu Benjamin and the late Iris Freeman. However, as fans know, Shirley Bassey has a natural ability to electrify an audience and command a stage. There is the remote possibility that Shirley's apparent regality and aloofness to former friends may have been inherited from royal status in her father's line. Although her Calabar father was a humble fireman aboard ship, his surname is found among the names of Nigeria's royal families. "Four Nigerians visited Britain in late May and early June 1913… These visitors from Calabar were 'on a mission of protest to the Colonial Office' over 'ancient rights of the natives'. They had royal status — Prince *Bassey* Duke Ephraim was the successor to the last *king of Calabar…*"[3] (emphasis mine).

Henry and Eliza Bassey raised their entire family at 182 Bute Street.[4] In addition to Shirley, who was the youngest, the family included: Iris and Ella, the eldest sisters, then Gracie, the twins Eileen and Henry and Marina. Further up Bute Street was another street in Tiger Bay where the Bassey family also lived prior to its move to Splott. On the corner opposite Herbert Street, at the base of a hill over the bridge which led to town, was a very small post office. Its front door once stood at the entrance to Wharf Street, which after intersecting Hope Street led on through to East Canal Wharf. In the middle of this narrow street, built mostly of warehouses and other such business premises, were a few terraced houses. One of these was the Bassey home, where Maureen Jemmett remembers often visiting to play with Marina. Ironically, the statue of the Marquis of Bute — recently removed from its ancient pedestal at the monument end of St Mary Street and placed in a new square designed to link the centre of town with the new Cardiff Bay — has been resituated almost on the very

In the foreground is Ella Lydon, elder sister of Shirley Bassey, with friends Bela Freeman and Beatrice Sinclair at the Butetown Community Centre's Senior Citizen's Club.
(Photo courtesy of the Sinclair family)

site of Shirley Bassey's one-time home. Today, Wharf Street has been completely erased from geographic memory by the emergence of the new Bute Square (recently renamed Callaghan Square), which occurred at the end of the millennium.

When Shirley was a young child, the family were rehoused in Portmanmoor Road in Splott, but Gracie still bicycled back to the community every day. When Gracie died in America,

Phoebie Saunders recalled at her memorial service, held at St. Mary the Virgin Church a few years ago, that you could tell the time by Gracie who rode her bicycle from Splott each day to St Mary's School on old North Church Street in Tiger Bay. Although all of Shirley's siblings have moved from the Bay, they still live in Cardiff. Ella still visits the Butetown Community Centre for the senior citizen's bingo session which still takes place on Sunday afternoons.

St Mary The Virgin Church, Bute Street.

There were other talented female singers from the area besides Shirley Bassey — like Rohima Ali, Patti Flynn, Lorne Lesley (Irenie Spetti), Rosie Roberts, Selina Duncan and Mahala Davis. Singing Welsh versions of "My Heart Belongs to Daddy" and Gershwin's "Summertime" from *Porgy & Bess,* Mahala (pronounced Ma-hay-la) was the first black female artist to sing on television in Welsh during the early 1960s. Like Shirley Bassey's sister Gracie, Mahala, and many other Tiger Bay and Docks girls, married American GIs stationed at Air Bases throughout England. Before emigrating to the United States, many spent time in London, particularly around Ladbroke Grove and Westbourne Park, an area in many ways similar, then, to Tiger Bay.

As it does today, London offered a much wider array of places to go for entertainment than Cardiff. Mainly located in Soho, the hot spots that attracted Tiger Bay exiles of that time were the *Americana,* the *Sunset Club* on Carnaby Street which later became the *Roaring Twenties,* the *Flamingo* on Wardour

Street and the *Marquee* where Johnnie Dankworth and his jazz orchestra often played. In the Westbourne Park area was *Club 2*, the *Calypso Club* and the *Fiesta Café*, while many from the Labroke Grove community also went to the *Q Club* on Praed Street. Many people from Tiger Bay — like Mahala Davis, Maureen Jemmett, Dorothy Freeman and the bohemian Anita Foster, to name only a few — were resident in the vicinity of Westbourne Park, so visiting was like home from home. Going to the West End to Tony Harris' *Allnighters* (which was the *Flamingo Club* before midnight) on Friday or Saturday night was almost a ritual.

A Tiger Bay exile in London, much ahead of her times in 1958, Anita Foster of Nelson Street.

After all, where else would you hear Ray Charles sing *The Night Time Is The Right Time* in late 1950s Britain? Certainly not on the BBC, as far as I remember. As I made my way down the entrance steps into the *Allnighters* on Wardour Street, the Raylettes, his background singers, repetitively sang out *Sha Du Day* from the sound system — and for that reason I always arrived dead on midnight in time for a weekly cultural metamorphosis. Ray Charles' epistle to the night announced a major transition. At midnight, the *Flamingo Club*, famous in some London circles for its promotion of American jazz, transformed into the *Allnighter* nightclub. *Ronnie Scott's Club* on Gerrard Street, located near to the *Allnighters* on Wardour Street in those days, regularly featured Tubby Hayes and Joe Harriet. But, unlike the *Allnighters*, it didn't stay open until the wee hours, just before the Underground was about to open, when it was time to take your weary body back to your digs.

Nor did it offer, with its sit-down supper club ambience, the free-wheeling atmosphere that the *Allnighters* allowed or London's Georgie Fame and the Blue Flames, who provided his British rendition of the essential rhythm and blues element.

Unlike Tiger Bay, in London you were one among the millions. But once I descended the stairs into the *Allnighters*, on one of my early 1960s' nightlife visits to the big city, paid my ten shillings and passed the large photographs of Sarah Vaughan, Ella Fitzgerald, Dizzy Gillespie and other jazz greats, the world became more intimate.

"You're from the Bay!" Maureen Jemmett's voice resounded above the excitement as she detected the Sinclair resemblance in my face among the crowd.

"What you doing in London," she went on, as I approached the bar, which only served coca-cola and other soft drinks after licensing hours.

"Hey! There's Henry Bassey," she excitedly interjected, as Shirley's brother walked across the dance floor towards the stage. The next time I saw him to talk to was almost forty years later in St Mary the Virgin Church at his sister Gracie's memorial service. Oddly enough, he remembered that night so long ago in a London jazz club.

The Beatles and the Rolling Stones were yet to be discovered, although the then-unknown Mick Jagger was seen on the scene, sometimes on the stage at the *Marquee Club* on Oxford Street. Be that as it may, I lived and died to get into the *Allnighters* on Friday or Saturday nights, and if possible on Sunday afternoons. It was the ultimate escape for an Afro Celtic lad from Cardiff destined for the drab life masses of workers experienced in the factories of Great Britain at that time. To judge by the present day media's constant reference to the swinging 60s, it appears that the sophisticated, working-class, after dark London clientele that flourished in such places as the *Allnighters* in Soho's pre-1960s discotheque days has been relegated to oblivion.

Meanwhile in Tiger Bay, a Somali called Hassan and an Arab called Shybie, who opened the *Seven Arts Club* in Mount Stuart Square around 1958, followed in the tradition of earlier times by keeping a few venues going, as did Barbadian émigré Cyril Clark. At the same time, Annis Abram of West Church Street continued the tradition of nightclub entertainment by opening a number of venues in the area as well. In the late 1950s, presumably reflecting his family's Egyptian background, he opened the *Cleopatra,* just outside Tiger Bay on Custom House Street.

In contrast to the not too distant past, with its ninety-three-odd pubs on the corners of congested streets, in addition to its night clubs, Tiger Bay today sports only one pub: *The Paddle Steamer.*

The Docks, on the other hand, still has a handful, including the traditional pubs like *The Packet*, the *White Hart* and the *Ship & Pilot*, managed by Michael "Junior" Burrows. Compared with former times, the community is not nearly as exciting as it once was. The most popular places for locals are the latter pubs and the more recent *Baltimore* and the now closed *Yardarm*. These alone keep burning what remains of the Tiger's fire, while on the other side of the tracks, Cardiff Bay's Atlantic Wharf Leisure Village entertains the rest of the city as its 900 parking spaces fill to overflowing on most weekends.

Chapter Five

WESLEYAN MEMORIES

Looking east out of one of the oval-shaped windows of Cardiff Bay Visitor Centre, one is immediately struck by the quite attractive but somewhat exclusive housing development of Adventurer's Quay. Situated on a Grovesnor Waterside site at the edge of the Roath Basin near the Roath Dock, it commands a view of the entire waterfront. However, this was not the first time that a community had lived on that site. Quite by chance one January day in 1997, I was rather pleasantly surprised to discover this fact in the main foyer of the Capital Shopping Centre. While demonstrating a model of the Cardiff Bay area to the general public as a representative of the Cardiff Bay Development Corporation, I was approached by 80-year-old William Henry Cooper, who was born in the small community at Roath Lock House in 1917, precisely on the same site of Adventurer's Quay.

His father, after whom he was named, was the lockgatesman for the Roath Dock and actually worked out of one of the two lockkeeper's cottages which still straddle the unused lock gate entrance that today leads into Cardiff Bay's new waterfront lake.

Roath Lock House, where he began his long life, was comprised of six flats, three on each side all made of red brick. As was typical in those days, the toilets were outside, and there was also a wash house with boilers for the mothers to use on washing day. The flats were built alongside a wall that separated them from the cattle lairs, where cattle stock imported from Canada were kept. William remembered with amusement the time a cow pushed her nose right through his mother's kitchen window.

On Sundays, he and other neighbouring children would

walk through the dock across the many railway lines which scarred the terrain and where trains shunted back and forth. They also had to cross over lock gates and pass the Railway Police Station, where a few other cottages could be found, before arriving at Bute Street en route to the Wesleyan Methodist Church on South Loudoun Place, leading into the square. Although his family was not strictly Methodist, like others in Tiger Bay, they were ecumenical and attended various different denominations of the multicultural and multilingual community they ventured into.

View of the docklands that William Henry Cooper and other children of Roath Lock House had to cross to get to church in Tiger Bay. (Photo courtesy of BHAC)

At one time, among the multitude of languages spoken on the streets of Tiger Bay and the Docks, even the native language of Wales could hold its own. In fact, four Welsh chapels were built in the area to provide for the needs of Welsh speaking families. The small chapel at the Clarence Road end of Pomeroy street is one of the two remaining structures left in the community today. The other, which was previously known as the Siloam Baptist chapel, originally founded in Patrick Street in the Docks, is the newly renovated *Byddin yr Iachawriaeth* or Salvation Army chapel across the Clarence Road bridge at the entrance to Grangetown. As the other chapel in Loudoun Square was sufficient, the Bethel Chapel of Mount Stuart Square, although remembered for its strong Welsh community connections, was provided in 1858 for its English-language-only-congregations.

Walking up Bute Street from his office in Mount Stuart Square, as he passed Loudoun Square en route to his home at the Quebec pub on Crichton Street, coal exporter, ship-broker and Honorary Consul of Yugoslavia, Frederick Charles Moon remembered "seeing the beautiful houses ablaze with light and carriages stopping and men and women alighting in full evening dress." For the winter 1997 edition of *The Voice of the Tiger,* his grand-daughter Jayne Chamberlain recalled Frederick's reflections of the vibrant life surrounding

Olwen Blackman (left) and her friend from Barry Docks, Pricilla Ankara, at the south east corner of Loudoun Square Park. A portion of the Georgian architecture of the Bethania Chapel can be seen at the far right.
(Photo courtesy of Olwen Watkins)

the office where he worked in the Coal Exchange. His view into Loudoun Square would have also encompassed the Georgian architecture of the Bethania, the Welsh chapel on South Loudoun Place, where Welsh composer Ivor Novello once worshipped — as the memories of Hodges Row resident Muriel Edwards Haworth indicated in her contribution to Issue No 91 of the local magazine *Making Waves*.

A resident of Loudoun Square who could not speak a word of English until he was about ten was Welsh teacher Reverend Maxwell Evans, the son of a seafaring family from Cardigan town, now resident in Penarth. At the turn of the twentieth century, his family were regular members of the Bethania and St Mary the Virgin Church on Bute Street.

Today, English, Arabic and Somali are the languages that predominate on the streets of the Bay. Although there are some in the community who can speak Welsh, Blodwen Glasgow-Ibrahim was one of the last original Welsh speakers of Tiger Bay when she died in the mid-1990s.

On their way back from Loudoun Square, William Henry Cooper and his friends of Roath Lock House would stop in front of the Pierhead Building and sit on a huge canon. There they would watch the White Funnel Campbell Paddlesteamers as they departed backwards and then turned out from the bay towards the estuary.

As they were for the children of Roath Lock House, depending on the tide, departures and arrivals of the paddlesteamers were a daily event for many in the community . (Photo courtesy of BHAC)

Above his flat lived Mary Bails, who in later years reminded William that he was the only child of their small community to have had an accident. Apparently, at the age of seven, he fell in the Junction Lock, which now flows alongside the Grosvenor-Waterside-influenced Scott Harbour business complex. Fortunately, he was pulled out by a friend before the dock rescue service arrived on the scene. Much to his delight, the agile rescuer was rewarded with some money from William's father for this brave act. In fact, it was this accident that caused the family to decide to move to the new houses being built in Tremorfa during the late 1920s.

As regards the fate of the tiny community at Roath Lock House, sometime in the 1930s those old flats were converted into a kosher abattoir for the Jewish community — where Jewish doctors used to regularly visit to ensure that the meat fulfilled the requirements of Jewish law.

Opposite the Bethania chapel, the Methodist Church that William Cooper and his friends attended up the Bay, remains a topic of conversation even today. After reading a copy of *The Voice of the Tiger*, David Binstead, for example, shared his memories of the Wesleyan church which came flooding back after reading Ken Marshall's description of life in the old square.

"Ken must surely be the Ken Marshall who was an early member of "my" Life Boy Team (called Junior Boys Brigade nowadays) and later the Boys' Brigade," David wrote in his letter to me. "By the way," he continued, "he is dead right about the 'Wesaleyan'!" referring to the way locals pronounced its name. However, according to David, the chapel had ceased to be 'Wesaleyan' in either 1932 or 1933, the date of the Methodist Reunion and had become "Methodist," although it was still referred to as Wesleyan long afterwards. He remembered with affection Esther Sheriff, who lived in a house on the banks of the Glamorganshire Canal, recalling she was a splendid lady full of vitality who used to work at Ashtons the Fishmongers in the Central Market. Although some locals called her "Sister," she was, in fact, a lieutenant. His interesting letter, published in the fourth edition of the magazine, went on to say:

<blockquote>
The "Sister" was the full time Deaconess at the Mission who in Ken's time would have been Sister Mary Morton (I think). She was an absolutely first class Christian leader and she and Stanley Watson along with Mrs. Watson — always called "Ma" by the men — made a superb team and really had an impact on the area. We certainly did used to march the 'length and breadth' of the Bay — from Peel Street in the North where the band always stopped playing as we marched past the mosque to Patrick Street in the South. Believe me, this was quite a fair march if one was carrying a drum or playing a bugle — but we used to love it!

I arrived at the Methodist Church Coloured People's Mission Loudoun Square — to give its full title — as my mother was on the original committee set up to convert the Church — once the Methodist Church in Cardiff — into a Mission Church to serve its community, largely West Indian at that time. Because of the depression and also the operation of the Tramp Shipping Subsidy Act, many coloured seamen were stranded at Cardiff with no ship, no job, and no hope of returning home. Many of the men, of course, had settled in Cardiff years before. I was asked by the Watsons to help in the Sunday School. I think I was 14 which would have been in 1936 and things just went on from there and I became heavily involved.

During the War my mother (we lived in Llandaff) was an Air Raid Warden at the post in the front room of the minister's manse, next door to the Mission at no. 35 and I have many stories about that.

So my memories go back a long way and are still quite clear in the main. I wish I could remember the things my wife tells me now as well as I can remember all the events of nearly 60 years ago!

Before I close, one thing I would stress. I may have come from a different background but many of the boys I knew so well, were friends of mine. For that matter, some of the girls were as well! And I think the friendship was mutual. We had some great
</blockquote>

times together and certainly the Bay was a vibrant lively, friendly place...

The Wesleyan continued to be a focal point for community events when it converted into an ad hoc cinema — much to the delight of 1950s' youngsters. In addition to cinematic exhibitions, it also had an adequate proscenium for staging dramatic performances.

Then And Now was the title of a little known play that was put on in Tiger Bay during the early 1930s. Like magic, this play was brought back to life during a conversation with 91 year old Loudoun Square resident Doris Joseph, who remembered so vividly those "it was lovely" days.

In her twenties, Doris was a devoted member of the Wesleyan Methodist congregation in Loudoun Square. She and other members, including Esther Sheriff, Bert and Dolly Bray, Uncle Ned (Mr. Bovell) and Uncle Ben, among others were all members of the cast of the play. This was a *real play* produced by Reverend Stanley Watson and his wife, who had previously been missionaries in Africa. They wanted to do a play about their experiences in, and knowledge of, Africa for the benefit of people unaware of the situation and condition of people of colour during that time in the early 1930s.

Reverend Stanley Watson, who wrote the play Then and Now, *discussing church matters with Edward "Uncle Ned" Bovell, who appeared in the cast with Doris Joseph.*
(Photo courtesy of Hulton Getty)

Doris remembered that while they were dressing and

getting ready for the performance, Reverend Watson used to stand in front of the curtain explaining to the audience what the play was about.

Concerning the meaning of *Then And Now*, "at a certain time," Doris began to explain, "they were slaves and some man went there to change it — a big man went there." Then the play goes on "to show how it is now." Perhaps Reverend Watson was referring to John Wesley, the founder of the Methodist Movement, who also played a fundamental role in the abolition of slavery or perhaps to Granville Sharpe, another "big man" of the abolitionist period.

Behind that curtain, Doris recalled with pride her role in helping people to understand the conditions African people withstood.

"We were slaves!" she said, referring to herself and her fellow cast members. All dressed up in old clothes, she wore a ragged, half-torn dress and "old, old shoes." The cast were set about the stage sitting on orange boxes.

"When the audience sees us looking so pitiful they're going to say "aaaww,"" she whispered to Dorothy, Joe Brown's daughter, who played her stage daughter. And sure enough, as the curtain raised, her prophesy came true: the audience made an audible sigh!

Doris Joseph as a young lady during the 1920s.
(Photo courtesy of Doris Joseph)

"Don't ask me how the people understood what I was saying," she went on, "because I didn't talk in my 'proper way' I had to speak broken English!"

At one point in the drama, Doris had the opportunity to break out in song and sang *Nobody knows the trouble I see, Nobody knows my sorrow ... Nobody but Jesus*. Doris of course was well known at the time for her singing of spirituals, as Edie Bindin would be in later days.

Eventually, the play was staged at every Methodist Church inside and outside of Cardiff. "What precious memories. We loved it!" Doris glowed with joy at the retelling.

Like a number of people of colour, Doris Joseph, however, was not born in Tiger Bay. She only arrived there in the 1920s. The light of day dawned on her in 1904 in Bargoed — up the valleys. However, her memories of her early days begin on Gellideg Street in Maes-y-Cymmer, near Hengoed. Her mother, Agnes Everson, was a Baptist by faith, although in later years the family, which included two other sisters, May and Violet, attended Wesleyan Methodist chapels. Steve, her seaman father, came to Wales from Savannah, Georgia in 1901. He was an African-American and probably arrived in the Bargoed Taff Valley by means of the Bargoed Rhymney Railway which connected the upper portion of the Taff Valley with Cardiff. Doris remembers he wanted to take her to America but tragically, when she was quite young, he contracted pneumonia and died within a week, leaving her mother a widow with a family to raise.

"Do you know Caerphilly?" she said. "My father is buried in St. Martin's Church, you know."

By the time she was fourteen, her family had moved to Bedwas Road, Caerphilly, where Doris learned her trade in sewing. However, in those days there was hardly any work for young girls. She was compelled to join the ranks of the domestic service and worked as a servant for a few families in London. After some experiences, she much preferred to work for Jewish or German families, who treated her well, rather than for English ladies. Answering a letter advising her to come to London, her mother told her to write back and "Tell them you are coloured! Otherwise you will end up roaming the streets of London." A letter came in response indicating, "We don't mind what colour you are, just as long as you can do the work."

After her time as a servant, she returned to Wales and discovered that a childhood friend from the valleys had moved into Tiger Bay and since become Mrs Nelli Ford of Patrick Street. Doris used to go down the Bay quite a lot to visit her. It was on one of those visits that she found a job — "An ordinary job, you know, cleaning." But from that time on she never looked back. She lived in Tiger Bay ever since.

In the Bay she met and married Vandi Joseph, a Mende seaman from Sierra Leone and together raised two sons, David and Norman. Like so many other African seamen, Vandi Joseph and his half-brother James Roberts, great grandfather of Ryan Giggs, the celebrated Manchester United football player, settled down in Tiger Bay.

Doris's son, David Everson, known to everyone in the community as "Jokus," was born in 1937. Speaking about his mother, he informed me that despite the fact that he and his late brother Norman were

South view of old Loudoun Square and the Wesleyan Chapel in former days before being rebuilt as St Paul's after the 1960s demolition. (Photo courtesy of BHAC)

adopted by Doris and her African husband, he regards Vandi as his true father and Doris as his true mother — even though his biological mother was Doris' sister Violet, who at the time lived on old Angelina Street. This explains why he is white, while his parents are black. Being adopted by an African endowed Jokus with African "uncles," his father's brother and their countrymen, who all looked after him and called him the

"Pickin." They even spoiled him, making him the first boy on old Alice Street to get a bicycle. Sadly, in more recent times, on a number of occasions when someone has asked, "How's your mother, Jo?" he has overheard a few voices saying "That's not his *real* mother" — a comment that he finds unwarranted and painful. More so, it is a comment that offends and contradicts the legendary tolerance and racial understanding for which the community of Tiger Bay and the Docks has been renowned. Although not seen as often as before, due to her infirmity, Doris resided in Loudoun Square until she died and was buried from the St Paul chapel in 2001.

Today St Paul's, a modest structure by comparison with the old, majestic, grey-stone Wesleyan Chapel, continues to provide services for a much smaller, modern congregation. But it has also provided space for non-religious activities, such as those of *Butetown History & Arts*. BHAC once used its rooms during its formative days, before moving to its present location on Bute Street.

As David Binstead recalled earlier, his mother was an Air Raid Warden during World War II. Manifesting the Tiger's power and prowess, as Doris did, many of the women and, of course, the merchant seamen of Tiger Bay played an integral role in that conflict.

Chapter Six

OFF LIMITS

As the chapter entitled *That Reputation* demonstrates, folks in Tiger Bay have spent a lifetime defending their community's reputation from a slanderous myth and legend which successfully deterred otherwise respectable people from entering its confines. We still have to do so. In fact, statistically, *seventy five percent* of the people of Cardiff have never been down the Bay — if we are to believe a contributor to the letter section of the *South Wales Echo* in early 2000, who was alarmed at the fact that the National Assembly was to be built in Cardiff Bay.

There was a time when it can be truly said that the Tiger was caged: Tiger Bay was literally *off limits*. Signs were posted at the top of Bute Street and Canal Parade stating that this community was off limits to American servicemen during World War Two. Granted segregation of troops by race was practiced during those days under American law, perhaps this explains the motive for keeping them away from a community that knew no such practice. Or were the authorities of the day implying that Tiger Bay was such a dangerous place that even the American Army was afraid to go there!? One can only wonder.

In any event, the GIs stationed in barracks in Sully were segregated. So two separate camps were built for them. When off duty, however, both groups of soldiers were given the keys to the city. They could go anywhere in Cardiff *except* Tiger Bay! The one place, of course, where black GIs would have been very much at home, as their U.S. Merchant Navy comrades had been in earlier decades.

Signs at the top of the main entrances were not to deter those intrepid black soldiers from getting into the Bay as many often found refuge and comfort from the stresses of war in the homes of hospitable residents of the area. Some soldiers even went AWOL (absent without leave), surviving in hiding places along the canal bank. Local residents still recall finding them, keeping their location secret and even taking food over to them, until their inevitable discovery by the MPs. Maureen Jemmett and her sister Violet remember doing this for two such GIs who had taken momentary flight from the racial oppression they endured at the military camp. MPs rode in their jeeps around the streets of the Docks and Tiger Bay on a frequent basis in search of soldiers who had dared to slip under the *Off Limits* signs.

Not all were so unfortunate. GIs could ride on the floors of old-fashioned taxis while local people acted as legitimate passengers, riding right past the military police and into the community. Now, in those days every door had to be locked in case the enemy parachuted down. If you left your front door open, as was the custom, the fear was the enemy could run into your house and take over. So doors were locked. In fact, this is where the tradition of "Who's there?" came into fashion. Before the war, people simply walked right into your home, sat down amongst the family, and you could do the same in theirs.

Once the taxi arrived at the door, special vigilance came into play. Lookouts had to make sure the street or the square was empty. The front door would be flung open quickly and the GIs swiftly rushed into the passage with the door safely locked behind them.

An incident very similar to this happened to Vera Johnson née Roberts, a local Bay Girl who would also don a military uniform herself between 1942 and 1946 and play her part in the war effort. She was dating Hank Jones, one of the Black GIs she had met at a dance organised by the American military itself, while her older sister Joannie was dating Jimmy Stuckey, who would later become her husband. A canvass-covered military truck used to stop outside the Great Western Hotel at the bottom of St Mary Street to take Cardiff girls to G40 in Sully, where these military dances were held.

Any local Cardiff girl could take her American beau home to meet her family — but not the girls of Tiger Bay as their homes were *Off Limits!* So Vera, in conspiracy with her other sisters, had to use the taxi method to sequester her GI and his fellow companion home to meet her mum. When they arrived in Loudoun Square the usual looking out was done and the GIs were safely escorted into Mrs. Roberts' house.

The military jeeps that the American MPs drove to patrol the docks also brought inadvertent tragedy to the community — as Cyril Actie had cause to remember of one day in 1942. A jeep rushed down old Angelina Street and accidentally knocked down his friend Vally, who lived on the north-east side near the home of James Ernest, the St Lucian father of Gerald Ernest and his brother, councillor for Ely Harry Ernest. Unfortunately, Valentine Frazier died of his injuries.

On a more lighthearted side, there were people in the community willing to betray all and community for a *Hershey* or an *O'Henry* chocolate bar or some other American candy. One such local tyrant was a very young rascal nicknamed *Tommy Tucker* by the local Bay Girls, who occasionally gave him what for! Hiding in an air-raid shelter, spying out for GIs was a lucrative trade for our *Tommy*, since he was never known to share his booty. Sometimes from his lair he could be seen puffing on a pipe. Since Mr Hassan, his Somali father, was not known for smoking one, he probably borrowed that pipe from the African seaman who lodged with the Hassan family household on Christina Street. In exchange for his sweet booty, this unscrupulous lad enjoyed riding as a mascot on the edge of the MP's jeep, gleefully pointing out the different houses where GIs had been seen to enter.

This fate was to befall Vera's home while Hank Jones and Jimmy Stuckey were in the house. A loud bang came at the door. No problem really because Vera's younger sister Winnie was well trained.

"Who's there!" she shouted out.

"MPs, mam. We have reason to believe there are GIs in this premises," said the voice through the door.

"No there's not!" said Winnie with much authority.

"Well can we come in and see?" asked the MP.

"I'm only ten years old and I'm on my own," said Winnie. "And my mother said I'm not to answer the door until my parents come home."

"Oh, I see," said the MP. "That's the right thing to do girl."

The marriage of Somali seaman Mohammed Hassan and Katie Link, the parents of the entrepreneurial Tommy Tucker. Circa 1920.
(Photo courtesy of BHAC)

When Winnie heard the jeep door slam she gave the all clear.

For the moment everything was OK. The next big problem would be getting them out safely. When that time came, Vera's older sister Joannie went all the way down Loudoun Square to the open bomb site, where eventually the Gypsy fair would come, brightening up the cooler October nights with its colourful lights, swings and roundabouts. The *Paddle Steamer* Pub stands there now. In those days, it was an entrance into the canal and you could walk along the banks of the canal all the way into town and of course outside the perimeter of *Off Limits* Tiger Bay. From the end of the square Joannie was flailing her arms about to indicate it was all clear. With the signal Vera and the two GIs ran swiftly down to the canal entrance.

Unbeknown to all, the jeep was hiding at the other end of Loudoun Square on the canal bank close to Canal Parade. It sat in the dark with its headlights off. In the meantime, our intrepid adventurers were stumbling along ever vigilant when suddenly the headlights came on. In a flash, Jimmy Stuckey leapt over Mrs. Dixon's back garden wall, knocking some stones off in the attempt, and dashed into the house to safety. Hank Jones, on the other hand, fled back into Loudoun Square so fast that Mrs. Roberts, who was talking to Mrs. Best at the time, remarked:

"Did somebody just go by!"

GI Hank Jones fled into the open front door and safety of Mrs Roberts house as the MPs scurried around thwarted once again from gaining their quarry. When Mrs. Roberts went back into her house she was unaware that someone was in her living room. When she looked inside "there he was, *rigid as a bottle of milk*," as her turn of phrase described him. Amusingly, in that very same room, Vera kept a pure white canary which had a partiality for one particular song.

"Put Joe Williams on!" Jackie Chambers often requested, because the moment Vera put that 78 record on the wind-up gramaphone, the little African bird would burst into song as it heard *Every Day I Have The Blues*. Incidentally the Winnie in this story is Winifred Wani Roberts, who would eventually become the mother of Welsh rubgy player Danny Wilson father of Ryan Giggs.

The Second World War, of course, had its serious side and, like many a city and town throughout Great Britain, the conflict in the sky rained down upon Tiger Bay. In its attempt to destroy the port of Cardiff, the *Luftwaffe* often missed targets and hit buildings along Bute Street and other areas within the community, including Loudoun Square. Olwen Watkins remembers the time an enemy plane flew over Tiger Bay, strafing bullets across her back garden. She does not recall hearing the sound of the gun fire so much as sighting the puffs of smoke the bullets made. Her Irish granny, quite deaf by this time of her life, could not understand why her black daughter Lydia was suddenly hustling her out of danger into the house. Unaware of the incident at Olwen's, Rita Delpeche née Hinds recalls seeing the same plane flying low over Christina Street.

Meanwhile, as the war raged, — the Bay being a merchant navy community — news would soon come home of losses at sea. A loud thumping emanated from the front door as Olwen stood in the passage of the large Loudoun Square house she once lived in. Wondering who was there and too small to open the lock, she stood on the wooden ledge near the base of the door which enabled her to reach the latch and open it.

Blocking her view of the spacious park outside her front door stood her auntie Ray. Looking quite flustered, Rachel Farrah was in a dreadful state as she rushed into the house holding her hands to her face looking for Olwen's mother.

"The Tacoma Star has gone down!" she yelled hysterically at Lydia as Olwen noticed the tears pouring through her auntie Rachel's fingers.

"Duallah," exclaimed Rachel as she began to list the names of the local seamen on board who were now lost to the community forever. Staring up at the adults, her fear increased after recognising the first name, because she had been so fond of that extremely dark complexioned Somali seaman who often frequented her home.

Simon Johnson — father of councillor Betty Campbell — Wilmot Young, and George Sango of Hodges Row suffered a similar fate when a German submarine sank the *S.S. Ocean Vanguard* in 1942.

Many local seamen were also on the Russian Convoy including Louis James, my father Walter Sinclair and his brother Thomas — to name but a few. Fortunately, the men mentioned came home to tell their stories. While we suffered losses at sea, local Bay Boys were also in the

Rachel Farrah (l) embracing daughter Lucille with Joan Freeman (r) and other friends. The very same Auntie Ray who rushed to Lydia Blackman's door bringing the tragic news of the sinking of the S.S. Tacoma Star. (Photo courtesy of the Sinclair family)

air — including radio operator John Actie, pilots Charles Taylor and Arthur Young, and navigator Alfred Grant. Charles Taylor was shot down over France in 1944, at the time of my birth, and Arthur Young, brother of cabaret chanteuse Patti Flynn, suffered a similar fate when his plane clipped a chimney pot over the town of Salford near Manchester in the north of England.

Sgt Arthur Young, wireless operator during World War II. (Photo courtesy of Silda Sinclair)

Son of Jamaican seaman Wilmot Young and his wife Beatrice Maud, Arthur, who was born at 30 Maria Street, joined up in 1941. Aspects of his training as a wireless operator and his service career have been recorded on page 25 of Joe Bamford's book *The Salford Lancaster*. By coincidence, the author of that book was one of Arthur's military colleagues and son of the women whose chimney pot Arthur's plane had hit.

"Sergeant Arthur Wilmot Young is

commemorated on The Runnymede Memorial on Panel 241," Bamford mentioned in his book, but was unaware that, shortly after his accidental death on 30 July 1944, Arthur was posthumously awarded his wings.

On the 4th of September 1941, on the occasion of Alfie Ashton's wedding at the Wesleyan Chapel in South Loudoun Place, a group of Bay Boys posed for the photographer. Bob Turner, one of those in the group, whose camera was used to take the snap, identified "George Morocco, Eddy and Julius Edwardsen of Sophia Street, Charlie Taylor, Arthur "Baldy" Perks, Ernie Shaw, Ritchie Ramos and Billy Nichols of

Bay Boys (L to R) Charles Taylor, Julius Edwardson, Billy Nichols, George Morocco, Ernie Shaw, Ritchie Ramos, Bob Turner & Baldy Perks. Taken on South Loudoun Place in the 1940s after Alf and Rosina Ashton's wedding. (Photo courtesy of Bob Turner)

Newtown" as the other members. After Rev. Watson married Alf and Rosina that morning, the bridegroom had to leave Cardiff that very evening to join a ship in Manchester. Charlie "Tala" Taylor of Angelina Street became a Flying Officer/ Bomber and was shot down in France while on a mission during the night of 2/3 June 1944 over Amblin Court, where he is buried.

Ritchie Ramos, also of Angelina Street, was at the time of the photo awaiting call-up and eventually served in the Middle East and Greece. Arthur Perks of Christina Street died in equally tragic circumstances. Having been partially crippled in one leg by polio contracted as a child, he was rejected for further service in the Merchant Navy, it being deemed a risk to have a seaman with such a disability aboard in wartime. So Baldy prevailed on the doctors to allow him to undergo a very long and painful operation in an effort to alleviate the handicap. This it did sufficiently for the Federation doctor to pass him fit; although he was told he could quite legitimately do his bit in the war-effort by remaining ashore in a civilian occupation. But fate would have it that the first ship he joined was destined to be sailing in convoy to Murmansk. Baldy, like so many others on that run, did not return.

In correspondence with me in my capacity as editor of *The Voice of the Tiger*, Bob Turner believed that he did not have the honour of being born a Bay Boy. But "from the mid 1930s onward," he said, "I spent so much time in the homes of my Bay friends that many people thought that the Bay was where I actually lived. So perhaps I may humbly claim to have been an honorary Bay Boy." No Bay Boys would disagree with him.

As most residents know, Mr Wesley was until his recent death one of the "old men of the Bay." Like so many others, it was the sea that brought him from Africa to Tiger Bay. Born Doe Wesley in Monrovia, Liberia in 1914, he has become known to everyone as John D Wesley. His people, the Kru, are known in Africa for their boating skills, so it was inevitable he would become a seaman. And once he had taken to the sea, his home port became Tiger Bay. His Merchant Navy Service Record indicates his shipping record began in 1944 and ended in 1973. He made a total of fifty-five voyages and he had a

Merchant Navy Cook's Certificate. During the Second World War, Mr Wesley's ship, the *S.S. Gari Gari,* which he boarded in Sierra Leone, was torpedoed just three days out from Gibraltar on its way to South Africa.

Surprisingly, it was only in 1989 that Mr Wesley received the three medals he earned during that conflict. These were the 1939-1945 Star, the France & Germany Star and a silver War Medal 1939-1945.

In stark contrast to the contributions to the war effort made by people of colour, particularly those from Tiger Bay and the Docks, what happened to some of these courageous men in the aftermath of war should not be ignored. What happened to James Augustus Headley after World War I has already been mentioned in Chapter Two, but as Neil Evan's research indicated, prior to that time, "A more sinister aspect of the wartime experience was a generalised hostility to aliens, encouraged by the general governmental policies enshrined in the Alien's Act of 1914."[1] Exacerbating matters even more, "Much of the press emphasised the alien presence in south Wales, particularly in its reporting of court cases."[2]

By means of this Act, racism was institutionalised. But black seamen rarely, if ever, spoke to their families about the consequent indignity. For example, it was not until the 1990s that Marcia Brahim-Barry, daughter of a Malay seaman and one of the founder members of the *Butetown History & Arts Centre,* became aware of this outrageous historical circumstance. She then interrogated her older brother about why he had never told her about this inglorious treatment.

As 1914 saw the Alien Act instituted, preventing black seamen from finding work on white British ships, so 1925 saw the enactment of the Alien Registration Act which further restricted even British-born blacks from acquiring work. These acts of discrimination would have an effect on the families in Tiger Bay who were supported by these seamen. Thus Moses

Hassan, who we shall meet again in chapter nine, remembers how his father Mohamed Duallah Mohamed wrote many letters to politicians about employment discrimination, the 1925 Order and, as a Somali, the independence of his country. Author Jeffrey Green, in a footnote to his *Black Edwardians*, expressed his indebtedness to "a Cardiff sailor turned musician who recounted the contempt he received when visiting the shipping office to collect his father's wages in the late 1920s."[3] The Cardiff sailor was Joe Deniz, one of the musical Deniz Brothers mentioned earlier in *Natural Barriers*.

Revealingly, Neil Evans also demonstrated that:

> In the 1920s black newcomers into Cardiff faced unrelenting hostility from the local authorities and the trade unions. The absence of overt riot is misleading here, for there were far more effective ways of continuing the process that had begun on the streets in 1919 into the post war period. Inverting Clausewitz we might describe it as the continuation of war by other means. … [T]he publication of a hostile report by the Chief Constable on the black population of Cardiff in 1929 … pointed out that people remembered the events of 1919 and feared that they would not retain equality of opportunity at the end of the war. They were right to be concerned about the way that blacks were treated in south Wales. Colin Holmes, the most knowledgeable historian of the experience of immigrants and minorities in British history, after discussing the registration of black British seamen in Cardiff under the Aliens Order in 1925, concluded: "Viewed in a sober historical perspective there are few clearer cases of the institutional oppression of minorities in early twentieth-century Britain."[4]

In *That Reputation,* it was suggested that the negative myth of life in Tiger Bay was a psychologically suppressed camouflage for the racism endemic in South Wales at the turn of the twentieth century. Evidently this camouflage continued until well after World War II.

After reading *The Tiger Bay Story*, Lord Callaghan "was

very glad to see the observations towards the end of the book about racial discrimination and its adverse impact on those who suffered from it." In particular, Callaghan passionately remembers an incident involving John Actie of Christina Street:

> He had been a radio operator flying with other members of the crews in Lancaster bombers which set out for Germany every night and were in terrible danger from the German air defence. He came to me shortly after he had been discharged from the RAF and told me that he had applied for a similar post as a radio operator to the British Overseas Aircraft Corporation, but had been rejected, despite his excellent qualifications.

> I took the matter up with BOAC but could get no explanation from them. I was extremely indignant because until then I had not come across racial discrimination, but I suspected that this was the reason his application had not been successful. Eventually I approached the Minister of Civil Aviation personally and had discussions with him. He also took the matter up with BOAC and finally I was given the very unsatisfactory explanation that Mr. Actie would not be accepted as BOAC would not allow mixed crews. The reason given was that in certain overseas destinations, coloured men were not admitted to the hotels that the crews occupied and they regarded it as necessary always to have the crew staying together.

> You can understand, as a young man who had not previously encountered racial discrimination, how indignant I felt about this and it has influenced my approach to matters of race ever since. Mr. Actie was both hurt, disappointed and enraged. It took him some time to get over the fact that the country had been ready to use him during its time of peril to fly dangerous missions to Germany but could not give him a proper posting worthy of his qualifications once peace had broken out.

Before politics would take our local member of parliament away to eventually become Prime Minister, James Callaghan, who maintained close ties with Tiger Bay and the Docks, did see John Actie become an insurance agent.

One who years later was fortunate never to experience racial prejudice throughout his military career was Roger Christian, a lad who grew up on old Maria Street. Like Doris Joseph, who I discussed in *Wesleyan Memories*, Roger was not born in Tiger Bay. Many people of colour in the community were, in fact, born in the valleys or coastal towns of South Wales — as was Betty Richards, the daughter of a Jamaican who came to work in the mines of South Wales on the eve of World War I. Born in Neath in 1916, she was one of eight children. After it was reported that her husband had died after returning to Jamaica, Betty's mother died of a broken heart. The report was false, but without parents Betty and her siblings were placed in an orphanage. In the 1950s, Betty eventually made her way to Tiger Bay, where she married local character Roy Jenkins. She has lived there ever since.

Roger, on the other hand, took his first breath during that Second World War as Kathleen, an Irish mother about to give birth to her second child, feebly climbed onto her kitchen table somewhere in Llanelli. Marlene, her six year old daughter stood fearfully by as her mother cried out in pain in this makeshift maternity ward.

While his daughter witnessed the birth of her brother, somewhere on the Continent, in the throes of war, the women's husband was blissfully unaware of this new addition to his family. This would have been the beginning of an ordinary life except for the fact that the father of *this* child was an African-American serviceman stationed somewhere in South Wales.

Without understanding, the little girl detected great fear in her mother's eyes as she became overwhelmed by the realisation there was no disguising the awful fact of Roger's appearance. Nevertheless, this was her child — and a beautiful one at that.

Ten months passed between his birth and the arrival home of the distressed mother's husband. Suddenly, this erstwhile soldier found himself confronted with the problem of having to accept the raising of a child that not only was not his but was also black. Given the mid-century conditions in a small town like Llanelli, he inevitably gave the mother an ultimatum: either the child goes or he does.

As it was, his mother left her husband, but not before fostering Roger to one member of the family after another. In any event, after a stay in Nazareth House in Swansea, there was only one place in Wales where Roger would be accepted. That place was Tiger Bay — as Lord Callaghan recollected in Chapter Four, when he recalled Flori Fernandez, who took in Phil Edwards, *in the customary manner that so many people in the Docks and Tiger Bay did.* Roger was finally adopted by Geane "Ginny" Christian, who lived on Maria Street (pronounced "Mariah") in Tiger Bay.

Mrs Christian, a white women of 42 years, who could speak Arabic fluently and several other languages including Russian, used her skills as an interpreter at the Cardiff law courts. Others in the community like "Algiers", the Algerian-born multilingual Mohammed Lounes, also assisted the police as a translator with foreign seamen who did not speak English. In typical Tiger Bay fashion, Algiers raised Alan Sestanovich, from the age of two. And he later resided in

Roger Christian, aged 5, at his Maria Street home in Tiger Bay. Circa 1950.
(Photo courtesy of Hulton Getty)

Hodges Square, where the police often brought seamen for his linguistic services. Like their father, the children of Alan Sestanovich, originally of Yugoslavian descent, still live in the area.

With regard to Roger, his adopted mother Ginny Christan had herself been an orphan who ran away at the age of sixteen and eventually married a black seamen named Johnson. However, before any children were born, he died and later she married David Christian. Before adopting Roger, she had already taken in Jean Massey, another mixed-race child who had returned to her family on Portmanmoor Road in Splott.

Roger was four when he came into Tiger Bay life to become Roger Christian. Eventually, we became friends. As our friendship grew, I gradually became aware that Roger was severely beaten virtually every day of his childhood. As my parents had never raised a belt or cane to punish me, this revelation of life was quite a shock.

Why she treated him so cruelly may have much to do with Ginny's own orphaned childhood. Were it known how she herself had been raised, perhaps this would shed light on Roger's difficult beginnings. Nevertheless, he was fortunate to find himself in a caring community such as Tiger Bay in the 1940s and 1950s. All the love he needed came from his neighbours, like the Abdullahs, the Pines and the Duarts, among so many others.

Roger left home at the age of fifteen to live independently down the Docks and, in an effort to avoid getting into trouble in the streets, he joined the army two years later in 1967. He would spend the next twenty two years in the Welch Regiment and the Royal Welch Fusiliers.

In later life, he was to learn something of his adoptive father David Christian from Berlin, the Somali-born owner of the Milk Bar on Sophia Street:

"What's your name, boy?" said Berlin one day.

"Roger Christian," he responded.

"Of course! I knew your father," Berlin went on, reflecting back to the time of the 1919 race riots.

"He went to court accused of cutting off the arm of a

Norwegian during the riots," Berlin said. "But he was released without charge."

Remarkably, in 1968, after being posted to Hong Kong by the Welch Regiment, Roger was once again confronted with the memory of his adoptive father. This incident occurred while he was sharing a room with his military comrade Rocky Lane.

"Is this your father?" said Rocky, while handing over to Roger the book he was reading. Detailing an episode in the life of poet, writer and literary legend Brandon Behan, who spent time at Hollesley Bay Borstal Institution, Roger read with fascination a passage from *Borstal Boy*. At the age of sixteen, its Irish author had been arrested and tried in Liverpool for being an agitator for the IRA and subsequently sent to a variety of reform schools. Intriguingly, encouraged by his housemaster to play rugby, a game which he had "always connected with the English or the upper-classes,"[5] Behan went on to say that Mr Shackleton:

> … put me playing hooker the first trial we had. I was like a streamlined bull at it, and there I played ever after. Jock played second-row forward and my two props were a big lump of a reception, a half-black man from Pompey, and in for croaking a judy [a woman] in an air-raid shelter, by the name of Lascelles, and another negro bloke from Tiger Bay, called Christian, the one [who] chopped the right arm off a Norwegian sailor with a butcher's knife.
>
> Sullivan, the screw, said that I was the whitest man in our front row.[6]

Instantly, Roger knew that this could only have been a reference to his father, David Christian, who Berlin had told him had cut off a Norwegian's arm. Not only did he learn that his father had played rugby while imprisoned, but also tried his hand at acting, as Behan further recalled being in a nativity play:

Chewlips and Jock and Tom Meadows were innkeepers and census-takers. Joe and I were picked for two of the Wise Men, and the third Wise Man, the Black King, was a real black bloke, who played in our front row at rugby. He was the bloke from Tiger Bay they called Christian.[7]

By 1972 Roger was posted to the author's troubled homeland. While patrolling in Belfast in Northern Ireland, he was shot in the back but fortunately survived. After his recovery, he returned to Wales and became a recruiting sergeant in Wrexham between 1978 and 1982.

As he was well capable of defending himself, Roger Christian never experienced racial prejudice from his soldier comrades throughout his military career — unlike the Bay Boys mentioned earlier. But there was one incident where his colour prevented him from serving the Queen.

Roger Christian in Belfast. Taken in June 1975 the day before he was shot. (Photo courtesy of Roger Christian)

"Why haven't I been posted to Buckingham Place?" Sergeant Christian asked his superior office.

"You know why. Why are you asking?" responded his major.

Even though racial prejudice prevented him from guarding Buckingham Palace, in 1975 he was able to defend the crown jewels at the Tower of London as sergeant of the guard.

The racial discrimination of the earlier wartime period did not only apply to men. Local Tiger Bay and Docks women were somehow confined to finding work in the rag factory, paper works or doing other "such dirty, dirty jobs."

Some of the women could not stand the stinking smell of the dirty rags at Sigman's rag factory. Nonetheless, their parents looked forward to the wages their children would bring home.

In the early 1940s, Vera Roberts, mentioned earlier as having eventually donned a military uniform, took her cards from the Labour Exchange to get one of the multitude of jobs that were going in Curran's ammunitions factory at the time. There were queues that stretched down Clarence Road with many girls, down from the valleys, all looking for work. The girls in front were getting their cards stamped as Vera approached for her turn.

"Sorry. No vacancy!" she heard.

Yet valley girls behind her managed to obtain work. It was obvious to Vera her complexion was too dark as she marched home in bitterness.

"I'll cut your legs off if you ever go to that place again to get a job!" said James Roberts. Vera's father was a proud Mende from Sierra Leone, who was rightfully indignant of the treatment his daughter received.

"Don't go there again! You hear gal!"

Never one to accept rejection, Vera decided to volunteer and joined the army in 1942. She spent the next four years serving her country. She was not alone in this endeavour as Betty Bourne, Ninah

Vera Johnson (front) on duty being inspected by the Queen's aunt, the Princess Royal, during the Second World War.
(Photo courtesy of BHAC)

Fettah and Francis Charles Macintosh of the Ford family on Patrick Street joined up with her. Other local girls followed them to assist in the war effort, including Nora Glasgow and Evelyn Dixon. Thus Vera was especially proud to be included in an inspection of her troop by the Queen's aunt, the late Princess Royal.

After her time in the war effort, Francis Charles Mackintosh of the Ford family, draped in traditional Welsh shawl fashion, buys fish from Tom The Fish outside Mark Levine's grocery shop at the top of old Angelina Street. The latter short, rotund shop owner often used to ask his young customers like Helena Boston who lived nearby: "How d'you like your ice cream. Hot or cold?"
(Photo courtesy of Hulton Getty)

Ironically, after she was demobbed, the Labour Exchange sent Vera to Currens for a job interview. She was compelled to go, otherwise her unemployment benefit would have been withdrawn. She went reluctantly and purely out of curiosity to see if she would be offered employment — which, indeed, she was. After explaining why, she promptly refused to accept it.

Sporting multi-million pound luxury penthouses and apartments today, the location where Currans ammunitions factory once stood is far from being *Off Limits*. Cleared away in 1999, the former site of the abandoned factory has been transformed into Century Wharf, a glamorous housing complex situated between the banks of the River Taff and the bed of the old Glamorganshire Canal.

Chapter Seven

ANOTHER RIVER OUT OF EDEN

In the title of a 1950s novel by Welsh author Jack Jones, which told the story of the rise of Cardiff as an industrial port, the River Taff was celebrated as *The River Out Of Eden*. As there was more than one river in Eden, this book would be amiss it if did not mention another waterway, "The Canal that Flowed by Tiger Bay," as I entitled an article I wrote for *The Voice of the Tiger* in 1994.

The Glamorganshire Canal, in addition to its importance to the industrial development of South Wales, holds special memories for many residents who grew up on its banks. It has already been mentioned in *Off Limits* how the Jemmett sisters came to the aid of hungry American soldiers who had gone AWOL and taken refuge *over* the canal, as the local idiom for "on the banks of …" would say. There is also the story of the late Josie Farrah, whose desire for a bicycle her parents could not afford became so great that she decided to "nick" one from outside a shop on Penarth Road. "Oh, the thrill of it all! At last a bike," she must have thought as she rode around the streets of Tiger Bay. But as tea time approached another rather ominous thought was to enter her head: what would her parents do when they saw the bicycle? As Josie was a bright girl, she didn't have to think for long. She wheeled her bike over to the edge of the canal and then promptly threw it in, having already found a piece of rope which she had tied to it. From then on, clever Josie was able to prevent it being *stolen* from her and could fish out her prized possession and ride it around the old streets until the day it rusted.

Well, that was wartime or thereabouts. Today, the old canal is a green stretch of land not well recognised by locals as Canal Park. Some youngsters are even unaware a canal was ever there! So what about its origin?

It was the rise of industry brought about by the Industrial Revolution that necessitated the building of the canals in South Wales. Thus, on June 9th 1790, Parliament passed an act to "make and to hold" a canal from Merthyr Tydfil through the bank near Cardiff in Glamorgan. In particular, it was the already established Cyfarthfa, Penydarren, Dowlais and Plymouth iron works in Merthyr Tydfil that brought about the development of the Glamorganshire Canal.

The Glamorganshire Canal as viewed from Tiger Bay toward St Mary Street in 1896. (Photo courtesy of the Central Library)

Thomas Dadford and Thomas Sheasby and their sons were the engineers who had designed and built the chief canals of South Wales. It was Thomas Dadford, the elder and Thomas Sheasby, the Younger, who were appointed to build the Glamorganshire Canal. In less than four years the canal was finished at a cost of £80,000. By 1799 an extension was added from the basin to the sea lock, allowing it to flow by what would eventually be known as Tiger Bay. This raised the total cost to £103,000. The site of the basin was clearly visible, complete with bollard, opposite the Central Hotel between the aptly named East and West Canal Wharfs until the year 2000 when

St Mary Street was extended through the old site to the newly created Bute Square.

The building of the Glamorganshire Canal was funded by the owners of the iron works and it is significant to note that the development of the iron works itself was made possible with the profits procured from the supplying of African slaves during the 1770s.

The canal ran from an approximate height of 600 feet down a 25 mile stretch from Merthyr through the valleys to the then small town of Cardiff. This led to the building of fifty one locks at various locations along its route. With the subsequent building of Cardiff Docks, and with the arrival of large numbers of colonial subjects, many of them African, settling in what was to be known around the world as Tiger Bay, we see that Africa had a profound influence on the funding and use of the Glamorganshire Canal, the most important canal in Wales.

Iron, limestone, bricks and wood were transported down the canal to Cardiff, but eventually it was coal that was to make the important difference to Cardiff as a docks and a city.

The canal itself wound its way through the city down to the sea, flowing alongside Cardiff Castle and under Queen Street. During the 1950s, somewhere near the modern Queens Arcade, you could still go underground and see the bed of the old canal running through a tunnel. Coming out of the tunnel, it then ran down towards Bridge Street, flowing parallel with and between The Hayes and Great Frederick Street over most of which St David's Mall now stands. At Bridge Street, there used to be an old iron bridge that crossed the Hayes en route to Bute Street. (It should be noted that the Hayes also used to be part of Bute Street at one time.)

The canal then ran along Mill Lane — where today we see the Marriott Hotel, and tourists and city residents enjoying themselves *al fresco* in the open air restaurants. At the Monument, located at the bottom of St Mary Street until the beginning of this millennium (when it was moved and transformed into the railway bridge entrance to the new Bute Square), was the canal's entrance into Tiger Bay. From there it continued its journey down to the sea and docks. This is the stretch of the canal that I remember so well.

Another early view of the canal as it flowed down Mill Lane where the Marriott Hotel stands today.
(Photo courtesy of BHAC)

On its southerly route to the sea, it branched off to flow eastwards into the West Junction Canal, which flowed just north of St Nicholas' Greek Orthodox Church. Prior to the 1960s' demolition, this area of Tiger Bay, between the church and the Great Western Railway, had a flourishing Greek and Cypriot community. It has subsequently been assimilated into the city at large, but at that time Nicholas Misangelos and his brother, who lived on Canal Parade, were close friends of mine throughout our childhood school days. At this juncture, perhaps we should arrest our journey down the canal to investigate at little more the Greek odyssey that took place in Tiger Bay.

Bute Square, the latest development designed to bring fresh business opportunities and commercial activities into the new Cardiff Bay, has transformed an area where land had remained derelict since the 1960s demolition of old Tiger Bay. St Mary Street now adjoins the new square, allowing city centre traffic congestion to spread into this one time residential area. In the past, however, Crichton Street and its surroundings were the heartbeat of a thriving Greek and Cypriot community, which also included Turkish families, forming part of the fifty seven or more other ethnic groups that made up the community as a whole.

St Nicholas Greek Orthodox Church originally built in 1906 still stands today and remains the main centre for the Greek Cypriot and Greek community in South Wales. (Photo courtesy of Betty Campbell)

In my school days, after meeting Zaneb, the daughter of Egyptian seaman Sonny Hamonda who lived on Maria Street, we would make our way up Bute Street to St Mary's Bute Terrace School. Passing the Greek boarding houses and cafés, we would meet up with Konstantine Gaugi and Georgie Georgatos. Marikie Tzivras would join us en route.

"Neilson Clair!" Marikie would call out as she saw me approaching her family's shop near the railway bridge. She never did realise that my name was just simply Neil. Mutual school friend Shirley Dangerfield would later reveal to me that Marikie, whose name is Greek for Maria, eventually died of a broken heart after the death of her beloved child.

The hub of Greek community life surrounded the St Nicholas Greek Orthodox Church. On reading an essay I wrote about the Glamorganshire Canal, which appeared in the winter 1994 edition of *The Voice of the Tiger*, Rev Father Anastasios D. Salapatas of the Greek Orthodox Community of Harrow was so impressed to see a reference to the old Greek community that he sent me a translated portion of his book *History of Hellenism in South Wales*. Part of this he permitted to be published in the summer 1995 issue of that same magazine. His story revealed that the "first recorded settlement of Greeks in South Wales was in 1873" and his literary submission went on to say:

> They came to Cardiff, and the other major docks of South Wales, because of the great industrialization and consequent activities in the ports at the time. It is well known how the Greeks and more especially the Greek islanders love the sea and the trade with ships, and this would naturally influence where they lived.

Archbishop of Cyprus, Cyril the Third, at the Consecration of the Greek Orthodox Church of St Nicholas on 6 May 1919. This photograph was taken outside the church at its southeast corner on Greek Church Street.
(Photo courtesy of Rev. Salapatas)

Interestingly, Mrs Selma Bowker also contacted me revealing that her grandfather, Babba Stratis Rousos, was, in fact, the first Greek ever to settle in Cardiff. He was the son of a fisherman originating from the island of Chios. One of her uncles had an office above the Kardomah Café in Bute Street, just south of Ship Lane down the Docks. For many years, he traded there under the name of "Ross Transport."

Of the early Greek community Rev Father Salapatas

related that:

> On 18 December 1873 we know that they gathered in Cardiff
> for the purpose of establishing an organised group, a primitive
> Greek community. They had with them a famous Englishman
> who had become an orthodox priest in Constantinople. His
> name was Fr Timothy Hatherly.
>
> A few years later, on 20 February 1876, the Holy Synod of the
> Church of Greece sent a letter to all bishops of the United
> Kingdom asking them to suggest that their monasteries give
> help to the building and maintenance of a Greek Church in
> Cardiff. Although the response to that is unknown, the official
> establishment of the community and the recognition by the
> Ecumenical Patriarchate nevertheless came in 1903 when the
> Holy synod sent a relevant letter to the community together
> with the first Greek Vicar Fr John Georgiades.
>
> The leaders of the community, all working on board ship or on
> the docks, knew they needed two more things, a church
> building which they built in 1906 and a community building
> to be used as a vicarage and Greek School, subsequently built
> in 1915.
>
> Although it was in 1989 that the freehold was eventually
> bought by the community, the land on which the Church and
> community building were built was initially a 99 year lease-
> hold obtained from the then Marquis of Bute. By 1910 the first
> constitution of the community was approved by a general
> meeting of the members and verified by the then King of
> Greece, George the First. With some amendments, it was
> published in 1914.
>
> The consecration of the church on 6 May 1919 was the next
> great event for the community. Cyril, the then Archbishop of
> Cyprus, at the time in London for political talks on the future
> of Cyprus, was invited to consecrate the church and he agreed
> to do so.

Many people, it should be mentioned, helped in establishing the community during the first 20 years of [the twentieth] century. Ship owners, ship captains and ordinary seamen gave money and brought certain articles from Greece, Italy and Russia for the church.

The Minutes of the Community Council Records show that the first priests also offered a great service to the Greek people of South Wales. They helped both spiritually and pastorally and also assisted them in their efforts to build their church and community building. Furthermore, they taught in the Greek School and supported the newcomers to find jobs and get established in the area.

From time to time the community suffered because of certain divisions among its people resulting from political problems brought to Cardiff from Greece. Especially during the difficult years of the First Wold War and its aftermath. This was mainly because the Greek people have a real passion for politics.

During the years of the Second World War many Greek seamen had to stay in Cardiff because of the hostilities in Europe. Some old Greeks remember that the population of the community was doubled then. The Greek cafes in the Docks were full of these people, who for a long time were out of work, and sometimes arguments between themselves could not be avoided.

From the beginning until today twenty three vicars have served the community. All of them have worked very sincerely and substantially for the good of the people. One of them, the Archimandrite Gennadios Themelis (1917-1928) is the only Greek priest who died and was buried in Cardiff at Cathays Cemetery.

Archimandrite Iakovos Virvos (1937-1938) later became Bishop of Apameia, and Assistanat Bishop to the Archbishop of Thyateira. Also, Archimandrite Emilianos Timiades (1949-

1950) became Metropolitan of Silyvria.

Spread out over the whole of South Wales today, the Greek Orthodox Community numbers some 2,000 people. However, most of them still live in the Cardiff area. Until the decline of the previously great port of Cardiff, those Cardiffian-Greeks were all living in the Docks area around the Greek Church itself.

According to Rev Father Salapatas, "The Greek Orthodox Church of St Nicholas and the community building area are thought of as a Greek island in the middle of South Wales. All Greek Orthodox, even many Greek Roman Catholics, quite often visit their island and regularly attend the church services and the other social activities. A major reason for this is because they feel at home in the Greek surroundings. Their most important concern is to keep their Greekness, their faith and culture alive."

Visiting Greek priest in the early 1970s talking to a parishioner, a local Greek barber whose shop was located on Bute Street.
(Photo courtesy of John Briggs)

Although the church of St Nicholas stills serves the Greek community, the redevelopment of the 1960s forced the exodus of its members to other parts of Cardiff and its environs leaving the church somewhat isolated from the hub of life that once encircled it. Thus it is only on Sunday mornings, if you happen to be walking down Bute Street, that you will hear the Greek language spoken as it once was so commonly on the streets of old Tiger Bay.

One who tried to re-establish a community base in Butetown was Michael Polycarpou, president of the Greek Cypriot Brotherhood, but his negotiations with Cardiff Bay Development Corporation ultimately led nowhere. Discussions about a site in Mount Stuart Square dissipated while a potential building on Hannah Street recently burned down. By coincidence, as Rev Father Salapatas's metaphor describes St Nicholas' church as a *Greek island in the middle of South Wales*, Neil Sullivan, in the Abstract of his thesis, referred to in Chapter One, similarly describes the larger area of Butetown, in which the church is situated, *as an island with no sun*.

In the days when the vibrant buzz of sounds still emanated from the Greek and Cypriot cafés, the canal flowed on along the junction and went under Bute Street over to the East and West Bute Docks. Here the junction flowed parallel to the south of Herbert Street which led out of Tiger Bay into Newtown. This district was the heartbeat of the Irish community that developed from the 200 or so Irishmen whom the Marquis of Bute imported into South Wales to help build the West Bute Dock in the 1830s.

On the corner of Herbert and Bute streets, close to the no longer existant *West Dock Pub*, once stood the *Irish Club* run by Mrs Lynch. There were ructions galore there, which were kept in check by a one-armed bouncer. One time, Chief Constable Wilson wrote to Mrs Lynch that he would gladly give her an extension if she would kindly tell him *what time she closed!* Other streets leading off Herbert Street were Pendoylan, North William and Ellen Street where Jim Driscoll the world famous boxer was born. (It has even been claimed that the poet T. S. Elliot was actually born in this community but I have no independent proof of this). It was some of the relatives of Jim

Driscoll who owned the Dimlands, a pub on old Sophia Street. When Olwen Watkin's grandmother Annie lived on the same street she would regularly slip over the road to the Dimlands for a drop of stout with Mrs Driscoll. Years later the pub would become the Zawiya, a small mosque and Arab School.

In Newtown, I often heard my mother say, everybody was more afraid of the priest than the police — at least back in the 1920s. When Canon Hannon, who preached fire and brimstone at St David's Church at the junction of David Street and Bute Terrace, approached a humble terrace house, he did not knock. He just walked right in.

Along its course away from Newtown in the westward direction, the canal flowed into the Timber Float. To the children of Tiger Bay, this was a large, inviting lake to play on. However, hidden dangers lurked and many a local child lost its life there by falling into the lake underneath the timber logs that were tied together and already cut into rectangular and triangular shapes. During the 1950s, Gloria Gauci, a Bay Girl of Maltese descent, happened to fall into the lake, but fortunately for her Ronald Sinclair, an expert swimmer, was there to dive in and save her life. The timber was there not as a floating playground for local youngsters but for other purposes, one among them being to await the journey to the mining valleys to be used as props and supports for the mine shafts of the lucrative

Ronald Sinclair and Norman Sweet who daringly sailed to town on a makeshift canoe during the early 1950s.
(Photo courtesy of the Sinclair family)

coal industry.

From the Timber Float the canal continued its flow down to the sea, running parallel to Canal Parade, where there were several industries such as Novell ("Neville") Tubes or Farnells, the wooden ladder manufacturer. Opposite Farnells, near old Frances Street, lived Mr Dowbella, an Arab seaman, and his family — which included a lad named Norman Sweet. The latter worked as a marshal with my brother, the aforementioned Ronald Sinclair, at the Saturday morning cinema club. Their job was keeping other children in line. In those days when the canal still flowed through town, these two friends came up with an ingenious idea to save them the long walk to Queen Street. They made their way to the canal and over to the timber float through the alleyway at the side of Novell Tubes. Once there, they made a "twoer" by nailing two logs together to create a sea worthy vessel. And they sailed it up the canal, through Mill Lane and on through town, on their way to the Empire cinema. After the sing-song and the film show was over and all the kids were safely escorted out of the cinema into the back lane or onto Queen Street, the two lads would go back to where they had tied up their make-shift canoe and sail back home down the canal to Tiger Bay.

Before reaching the sea, the canal had one more detour to make before arriving at its final destination. That was at Hodges Row, the boundary between Tiger Bay and the community referred to as "The Docks" — although some include as part of Tiger Bay the area down to Patrick Street where Belmont Walk exists today.

Hodges Row was a small row of terraced cottages that led from Bute Street into the *Barrel Field,* where a basin was contained into which the canal flowed when the lock gate was open. Up until shortly after the second World War, people like the lady with an unusual gait known as "Boat Flo," lived on houseboats on that basin and alongside. Some people remember there were five or more cottages close to the water's edge, all painted white with roses growing around them. In one of these cottages, which had a large orchard behind it, there lived an old lady who was thought to be a witch by some local children. Despite their fear, some intrepid locals used to venture over there to buy lettuce and other produce from her.

Winning the video *A Stroll Through Tiger Bay* in a competition sponsored by local magazine *Making Waves* in 1998, triggered off a host of fond memories for Muriel Edward Haworth, a surviving resident of the old Hodges Row who is now in her eighties. Muriel, who lives in Splott these days, was born and grew up in Hodges House — now long since gone. Extracts from her memoirs published in the April 1998 edition of *Making Waves* indicates that William Thomas, her great-grandfather:

> came to Cardiff in the early 1800s and bought Hodges House from old Mr Hodges and ... set up a cooperage business.... He had two horses which were used to deliver barrels to the breweries.

She continued:

> We owned several cottages in Hodges Row. When he died, my grandmother Hannah Roberts and her brother William took over the business. It was a wonderful life.

Muriel's other grandmother, Sarah Jane Edwards, "was a district nurse and midwife, affectionately known as the 'Mother of all nations' because she went round delivering babies for everyone in what was already a multi-racial community. She used to walk [up the Bay] all the way from the Sealock Cottages [situated] down the Docks without a worry about her safety."

The army requisitioned some of the family's cottages in

Hodges Row "to park their trucks" during the Second World War and Muriel soon struck up a romance with a good-looking Lancastrian soldier serving in the 16th and 30th Welsh Batallions, which were stationed in Cardiff at that time. In 1941 she married Joseph Haworth whose "batallion was at Dunkirk at the time of the evacuation but, as he was ill with pneumonia, he missed it all and instead spent that period recuperating at 54 Bute Street." Her father also fought in World War Two and was decorated for gallantry.

Those were very happy days for Muriel but times changed and "aluminium barrels replaced the traditional wooden ones and the business closed down along with other businesses such as Jenkins Yard. Eventually Hodges Row was bought on compulsory purchase and demolished to make way for what is now Hodges Square."

Continuing our journey along the canal bank, one could see the capstans, some of which remain to this day, where many a barge was moored. At one time, these barges could transport twenty-four tons of coal.

Upon reaching James Street, canal traffic would have to wait for the swing bridge to open before continuing the final journey into the docks or out to sea.

Unfortunately, in 1951 a sand dredger called the *Catherine Ethel* accidentally collided with the inner lock gate releasing the canal water and taking everything with it onto a mud bank out in the estuary bay. The lock gate was never repaired and, for the subsequent years of its life, the canal became a tidal waterway, exposing its muddy bed each time the tide went out. This provided a dangerous adventure playground for local children to play in — if they dared to risk the wrath of their parents, should they find out.

It also provided the home for the few local down-and-outs or "tramps," as the homeless were referred to in those days, like Larboard, a man who, it is rumoured, came from a well-to-do background, or the old East African tramp, another who had fallen from grace who had been, unlike his country-men, a student and not a seaman.

"All the way home, Zamba! All the way home!" chanted local children, who taunted and chased after him, as he, long before my time, forlornly wondered the streets of the commu-nity and canal bank. One day, in the 1940s, he was found dead. There was also the colourful Saccharine. Saccharine Peters, the son of a West Indian coal miner and a Welsh mother, was born in Treorchy but was a well known character around the pubs and streets of Tiger Bay. Sometimes you might also see Swansea Kate or Emma Bailey sharing their methylated spirits together with some of those just mentioned.

Finally, in the early 1960s, the canal was filled in, bringing an end to its long and arduous but idyllic life. Meanwhile, life in the aging Tiger continued amongst its remaining residents — like the still-flourishing members of the Somali community.

Chapter Eight

SOMALI SAFARI IN A TIGER'S LAND

As the new millennium approached, the last decade of the 20th century brought an almost daily barrage of global conflict to the attention of a televisual world. Of the many horrendous scenes magnified by the media, the plight of the Somali people in Northeast Africa and the resulting refugee crisis had a particular impact on the community of Tiger Bay and its pre-existing enclave of Somali inhabitants.

In today's complex world, which has witnessed the Gulf War, the Bosnian conflict, the September 11th atrocity in the United States and the resulting Afghanistan War, divisions arise at the drop of a hat. Yet, in contrast, Tiger Bay, throughout its 150-year-or-so history, has been noted for its internal ethnic tolerance while it weathered many a racial storm that blew in from outside its confines. Until more recent times, it also managed to avoid the tendencies to which the rest of the world so easily seems to succumb. Despite the fact that the Somalis are not unfamiliar within this aging multi-ethnic community, even in Tiger Bay anxiety has arisen as a result of the growing Somali presence. Given these tensions and the continuing decline of Tiger Bay's old ways, a re-examination of the community's Somali history may alleviate some aspects of this rising social pressure.

Of the estimated 6,000 people of colour who lived in Tiger Bay and the Docks by 1945, some 1,500 were of Somali and Arabic origin. Somali people have been long associated with South Wales — since before the beginning of the twentieth Century. The research of Newport-born Ibrahim Ali, a founding member of the *Horn of Africa Charity* and a writer and publisher of Somali descent, has shown that due to the high demand for labour that existed just prior to the turn of the twentieth century, the Somali community grew quite prosperous in the region. He tells us that it:

> is easy to see why many Somalis left their homeland. The "Mad Mullah" [Muhammad ibn Abdullah Hasan — the Mahdi] was ravaging the country: law and order disappeared completely.

In fact Ibrahim Ali's grandfather died at the hands of the *Mullah* during that time of crisis. However:

> Before northern Somalia became a British Protectorate, the Somalis had a good perception of the "outside world." For example Burton on his way from Zayla to Harar (1854-5) was surprised to meet Somalis who had wandered through Arabia, India, and Egypt: "many speak with fluency three or four languages and are perfectly acquainted with English manners and customers." Interestingly, Burton also discovered that news travelled fast and learned of events in the Crimean War quickly after they had occurred. This was because Somalia had excellent trade links. The northern Somali port of Berbera drew a phenomenal income from trade. Towards the end of 1884, Berbera and Zeila were occupied by British troops, and treaties were concluded with all the tribes. Thus began the long association between Somalia and Britain.
>
> As would be expected, the Somalis who came to South Wales were all from northern and northeastern Somalia. As far as Cardiff and Newport are concerned, most sources suggest that the first Somalis in Cardiff arrived from South Shields — near Newcastle. Jobs were the main reason for the move. Some say that Somalis stayed in Cardiff and Newport because the weather was much better than in northern England.

Ali's account of early Somali migration to South Wales mainly concentrates on the establishment of boarding houses or tea houses, which formed the backbone of Somali life in Newport.

His account effectively describes how "They would all gather, playing cards and drinking tea — the smoky room always full of loud debating voices." These are common practices of the Somali community here in Cardiff. It was also the place where "Turub," a game with two opponents on either side that is similar to the Western card game of Poker, and dominoes were played. Those not playing usually discussed politics while others smoked hooker pipes or hand-rolled tobacco cigarettes.

As for our Somali past, we recently regretted the loss of Abdi Guri, who died at the ripe of age of 107 (though this was disputed by hospital officials) and didn't look a day over 80. Betty Hassan née Farrah says Somalis are good at hiding their true age! Alas, many a story has gone to the grave with dear old Abdi. If any one was ill, Abdi was there with one of his numerous medical concoctions to ease the pains.

Many residents can still recall spending their time at Berlin's Milk Bar on Sophia Street. The juke box in the front belted out the latest American Rock & Roll records like Bobby Freeman's *Do You Wanna Dance*, or the ballards *Silhouettes* by The Rays and *Could This be Magic* by The Dubs or the sound of the pulsating rhythm of Jimmy McCracklin's *The Walk*. In the back room you could sit down to the best curry and rice outside of the Bombay Restaurant on West Bute Street, which was owned by Nessar Ali, one of South Wales's first successful Asian businessmen. Of course, boy met girl at the Milk Bar: American GIs met Bay Girls there, and Betty Farrah met her Abdi there. Roy Hamilton's *Unchained Melody* was the song that did it, says she!

Abdi Hassan, Betty's husband, worked on the sea dredgers down the docks for 25 years, never signing on the dole in all that time.

"How long have you been in the country, Sir?" said a dole officer to Abdi when he eventually had to go there because work on the docks had begun its inevitable decline.

"You wasn't even born when I came to this country!" said Abdi to the bureaucrat.

"What you talking about! Why you don't look at my record? Why don't you ask me what I been doing? Not when did I come to this country!"

Abdi clearly demonstrated that he shared that Tiger Bay pride that residents customarily refused to let outsiders take away. Dignity was all!

Many still remember Yusef Farrah, known to one and all as "Cowboy" because of the ever-present cowboy hat which he wore everywhere he went. He married local damsel Rachel Holder and she became Mrs Farrah, the Auntie Ray who stormed Lydia Blackman's door to tell of the sinking of the *S.S. Tacoma Star*. (Farrah, of course, is a typical Somali name.)

At times many Somali seamen resident in Tiger Bay returned to their homeland — as did Omar Musa Hersi around 1927. He had planned to take Sarah Slapper Hersi, his Jewish wife, and their children with him. In fact, two-year-old Omar Musa and his elder brother, who were born in Nelson Street, were taken with their father while his mother and two sisters, Maliha and Stella, stayed behind with the intention of following later. If all went well, the whole family were to stay with their Uncle Ali Hersi in Las Anod in northeast Somalia. However, a tragedy at sea was to change all these plans.

Meliha Musa Hersi, one of the two sisters to remain in Tiger Bay while Omar and the eldest brother were taken to Somaliland in 1927.

(Photo courtesy of Hulton Getty)

On a particularly stormy day, Sarah sat in the front room of her Nelson Street home watching the rain when suddenly a tremendous flash of lightning illuminated the room. As she looked through the window, she was quite startled to see Musa in the light of the flash. Twice more the lightning flashed and on both occasions she saw the vivid image of Musa.

A few days later, she was confronted by two policemen, after answering their knock at the door. Ominously, she recalled her visions and, after a momentary loss of composure, she interrupted the officer who was about to speak.

"Don't tell me! Something's happened to Musa."

The police officers confirmed that her husband was dead and had been buried at sea. Although details were sketchy, it was known that his stomach had become extremely distended before he died. Because of a quarrel he was known to have had with other crewmen, Sarah believed that Musa's food had been poisoned, bringing about a tragic and untimely end to his young life.

Sarah's grief was compounded by her inability to get her two young boys home from Somalia. She did not have the money to bring them home. Even if she had been able, how would she take care of them and her daughters during those difficult days? In the course of time she remarried — another seaman — and moved to 204 Bute Street where together they raised four additional children, Betty, Jacob, Cecil and Sammy Smith.

Omar Musa in his early 20s shortly after returning home from Somalia where he had been taken to live in 1927 at the age of two.

(Photo courtesy of Elizabeth Musa)

Meanwhile, as the years passed by, Omar always wanted

to come home from Somalia. Eventually, he got the opportunity when a French Liner, transporting French, Nigerian and Senegalese troops to Europe, docked in Djibouti. He stowed away on board that ship and soon arrived in the port of Marseilles, France. Penniless, he was helped by a fellow Somali who, along with a lad from Aden, got train tickets for all of them to go to Paris. After a few days, Omar was on his way to London from where he telephoned an Arab boarding house in Tiger Bay to get in touch with the mother he barely knew.

Mohamed Duallah Mohamed, left, prominent member of the Somali community of Tiger Bay stands next to Paul Robeson. Taken in 1949, both men stand near No. 9 Loudoun Square where Robeson was visiting his African-American countryman Aaron Mossell. (Photo courtesy of Vera Johnson)

From the Cardiff General Station Omar took a taxi to the boarding house on Bute Street. After a neighbour went to fetch Sarah, mother and son were once again reunited. For a time Omar would live with his half-brothers and sister at 204 Bute Street, next door to the Seaman's Store owned by Lily Volpert whose tragic death in 1952 was mentioned in chapter two.

Undoubtedly, one of the most prominent members of the Somali community in Tiger Bay was Mohamed Duallah Mohamed, a self-taught man who fought tirelessly for the independence of Somalia from British colonialism. Another was Asker Farrah, who fought for the British in the Camel Corps during the first World War. At the turn of the Twentieth

Century, after settling down with his Cardiff born wife Clara and their children Raymond, Judith and Patricia and the already-mentioned Betty, Mr Farrah raised his family in his quite substantial, three storey Victorian home with cellar near the street lamppost on the north side of old Loudoun Square. His father-in-law Archibald Card was in those early days the owner of the *Bessie Anne*, a barge that was used to ferry the bodies of unidentifiable foreign seamen found dead in and around the industrial docks. (His involvement in this morbid task began in earlier days when cholera ravaged the South Wales community.) Generally, these unfortunates were taken to be buried on Flat Holme, an island which can quite easily be seen from Cardiff docks.

At one time, the back yards of the Farrah home in the square and our modest terrace house on Frances Street were back to back and thus I often saw Betty putting the washing out on the line. Of those days, Betty had fond memories which included seeing my brother Ronald up on the back garden wall fixing my mother's clothes line while singing the *Peanut Vendour* song, which was quite popular back in the 1950s. Back then, he would not have said: "There's a women of Somali descent." And likewise, she would not have said of Ronnie: "There's that descendent of Afro-Caribbean people." They were just Betty and Ronnie.

Betty Farrah, who is now deceased, often related to me how, when she was a teenager, long before she met Abdi, she used to coaxe her younger sister Judith to go out into the back garden to see if Ronnie was on the back garden wall. At her signal, Betty would rush out to put the clothes on her line all the while swooning after Ronnie.

Yes, we were that intimately connected, for the Somali people go back through time in Tiger Bay. As Betty says, "They paid their taxes and National Insurance" like everyone else. Did Mr. Farrah pay his dues for Britain? Unquestionably so.

Mr. Farrah was a veteran of both the First World War, the "Greatest War of Civilisation" as Betty described it, and the second. From the two world wars he earned the African Star, Pacific Star and the Atlantic Star. Many of our grandfathers won their medals in those wars. These should be among our family heirlooms but, as in the case of the Farrah family, the rag-and-bone man came in trying times and many of those medals were exchanged for children's balloons and other trinkets or for desperately needed cash.

There are Somalis still living in South Wales who fought in the Camel Corps in the North African Campaign against Rommel. These men were treasured characters of the old Bay and they are part and parcel of all our history in South Wales, where many of their descendants still remain today. In times past, Somalis were never seen standing around with the begging bowl, as they always managed to take care of their own. However, today they do stand in need of compassion and assistance. Under the guidance of Abdi Karim and many of the community at large, the *Somali Advice and Information Centre* and other organisations have been set up to assist new arrivals into the community. Like everyone else, they are struggling to survive. The Somali community has paid its dues to this society, thus their entitlement to help from social services is indisputable.

Cardiff's existence as a seaport encouraged men from the four quarters of the world to settle in the old community. Nowadays, particularly since the Somali crisis, more and more women have followed in the footsteps of their men and become visible in the area. As a *Dock's Girl*, Betty Farrah recognized the special needs of these women from her father's country. Before she died, she helped to form a Somali women's group and sought the help of NewEmploy Wales and the Cardiff Bay Development Corporation to provide facilities in Mount Stuart

Square where they could meet. These women held together what was left of families that have been killed and homes that had been destroyed. Many of their children have been maimed and left disabled.

"When they have taken care of their men and fed their children, where can they go to get away from it all?" asked Betty. She was concerned that this facility would provide a haven for them. As skilled craftswomen, Betty was enthusiastic that their handicraft and sewing abilities would be put to use, for example, around Carnival time in the making of costumes for the parade. To their credit, these women formed their own fund-raising committee and raised enough money to create a village for orphaned children in Somaliland. The Somali women received a great deal of support from Betty Campbell, MBE, and the children of Mount Stuart School who had a jumble sale in aid of the orphaned children. Sadly, Betty Farrah passed away before many of her dreams for these women could be fulfilled.

Somali youngsters in the Bay also need a place to express themselves in their own cultural way. Since some of them are suffering mental problems derived from the conflict at home, and many are turning to excessive use of ghat, a mild intoxicant, to solve their problems, there is a need for a centre for the Somali community.

Exacerbated by the conditions that set in within the community while the Cardiff Bay Development Corporation improved the surrounding areas, the resulting dereliction has placed undeserved pressure on what remains of Tiger Bay's harmonious spirit. On the 10th April, 1998, for example, a great tragedy unfolded that might have come out of the ancient pre-Islamic epic of Arabic literature *Layla & Guyïs*, a story more familiar to us as *Romeo & Juliet*. Driving into Loudoun Square towards my garage that afternoon, after completing a special Tuesday History Walk around the seafront, I found myself

obstructed by three vehicles, an unoccupied car in the middle
of the road, an ambulance and police car. Quickly manoeuvring
my way around these obstructions, I came close to the curb,
which was lined with onlookers most of whom were young
Somali men. From what I gathered from them, there had been
an accident, a fight, but beyond this I could get no specific
details.

*Muslims celebrating Eid (Arab Christmas) in the mid 1930s — marching from Bute
Street along South Loudoun Place, approaching the railings of the Bethania
Chapel on the corner of Loudoun Square. This photograph was bought by Caroline
Fairclough from a box outside a bookshop in the Westminster area of London.
(Photo courtesy of Vanessa Davies)*

Being *Arab Christm*as as they say in Tiger Bay, or more
correctly Eid, that same day was also the holiest day in the
Islamic calendar. Thus when I entered the rear entrance of the
Loudoun Square flats, many Somali women in traditional dress
were congregating there. To enter, I had to squeeze my way
through — while exchanging the traditional *Eid Mubarak*
greetings. It was only then that I got an idea of how serious this
accident had been. Before I got into the lift, a very young friend
of mine gave me the gory details of how someone smashed the

window of the car with a stone.

"There was lots of blood," said Sulayman, a diminutive lad of Yemeni descent. As he uttered these words, excitement burst from him. I presumed that whoever had been injured was being taken care of inside the ambulance. Seeing the news on television the following day, I soon discovered that Faud Abdi had died in that accident. Only then did the full impact of the tragedy register.

Reporting so early after the incident, the media was inexact about the facts. It happened in the Loudoun Square Estate, they said! And as announced on the Welsh language news: *Fe ddigwyddodd y digwyddiad ar gyrion Bae Caerdydd!* That is, it happened on the edges of Cardiff Bay! Early versions of the story, adding spice to the occurrence, were intriguingly peppered with the drug taking overtones of ghat consumption. Evidently, unpleasant problems, when subjected to media representation, are placed outside the confines of *Europe's most exciting waterfront development* — and, invariably, Butetown is identified as the trouble spot. Nevertheless the-still-beating heart of Tiger Bay is at the geographical epicentre of the new development and not at its boundary.

The remarks in the media concerning this incident showed a certain degree of cultural insensitivity toward the Somali community that has been resident in Tiger Bay for more than a century. In this case, a crime of passion was very much the motive behind this tragedy. Just as in *Layla & Gayïs*, a young couple fall in love and want to marry, and like the enmity between the Capulets and the Montagues, clan differences within the Somali community mitigated against this young couple fulfilling their desires short of running away — which is what they chose to do. They stole a moment of happiness. Word reached them that if they returned the girl's family would permit the marriage. This, however, was not the case and her brother sought to punish the man who stole his sister away, resulting in the unhappy events whose tail end I was to see in Loudoun Square.

By Tuesday, 1ˢᵗ December 1998, when the case was brought before Cardiff Crown Court, the *South Wales Echo* would reveal:

> A YOUNG Somali college student was murdered in Cardiff
> after falling in love with the wrong girl.

This was common knowledge in the community long before then. Ironically, neither the assailant or victim of this crime were members of the local community but residents of Newport. This was nevertheless a great tragedy both for us and the Somali community as a whole, which deserved our heartfelt compassion.

Since its exit strategy brought the development corporation to an end in the spring of 1999, Tiger Bay has continued its gradual slide into deprivation and social upheaval. The Saturday evening, 27ᵗʰ August 2000, for example, would have been like any other, spent watching television with mam at home, except for the loud din that emerged from below. Depite being six flights up, the noise actually interfered with our ability to hear the *Inspector Morse* drama on HTV. It prompted me to get up and look out of the window toward the origin of this disturbance. As it was August Bank Holiday weekend, I initially thought I was missing out on some celebration that old Tiger Bay's fading grapevine had forgotten to inform me about. All I could see in the twilight was a large crowd of people gathered in front of Joanne Madden's *Paddle Steamer,* the local pub in the southwest corner of Loudoun Square.

Torn between going down to join the event or continuing to watch *Morse*, I sat back down on the couch. But the increasing din caused both mam and I to try once more to ascertain what was going on by peering out of the window. By now Councillor Betty Campbell had come out of her home as had many other neighbours. With my curiosity at an all time high, I decided to get down as quickly as possible to find out what was happening, particularly after police sirens could be heard in the distance.

"There's a riot out there!" said one of the two security guards, as I reached ground level and the rear entrance door of the lobby.

Although anything is possible these days, I could not believe at first what I was hearing. As I approached the debacle, I could see Mary Hassan-Saleh and Nino Abdi as well as Betty in the crowd.

"It's just kids," Mary said.

Indeed, the area was swarming with them. Where they came from was really hard to tell as there was so many unrecognisable faces. Saida and Nassia, two of the Suleman sisters, were among the adults outside the pub. I heard the unbelievable from Saida, as she described an ethnic squabble between local Bay and Somali youths. Some parents had even put their young ones into taxis and sent them home, away from the altercation. While I stood there, nothing serious was taking place. In fact, the two squad cars that entered the square from Bute Street had already left.

Never in the history of Tiger Bay has this community experienced internal ethnic discord on this scale. The 1911 riots that ultimately forced Cardiff's Chinese inhabitants to remain confined within our community boundaries and the 1919 riot, that did the same for Black people, were conflicts that were ignited outside the community. Ethnic dissonance between longstanding residents and Somali youth contradicts the traditional tolerance that made Tiger Bay what it was. Thus, it is extremely distressing to witness the beginnings of such fragmentary behavior within the community at the beginning of the new millennium.

As is the case in many other communities, there is nothing locally for the youth to do. Apart from the Butetown Youth Pavillion on Dumballs Road that caters primarily to younger teens, there is no youth centre in the area, as there once was in Loudoun Square, where they could be involved in more constructive activities. This is a generation which has been raised by a media that has brought ethnic conflict into our very living rooms. Perhaps they regard such conflict as normal behaviour.

It is pertinent to point out that this disturbance occurred four days after the publication of an article in the *South Wales Echo* entitled *Welsh Areas Reach Depths of Deprivation*. The article indicated that "Butetown is ranked as the most deprived ward in Cardiff," and concluded with Assembly Finance Secretary Edwina Hart saying, "This report represents a significant step forward in our efforts to identify areas of greatest need in Wales." We cannot disagree that this is a step forward with reference to the identification of the worst examples of poverty in the other twenty-one local authorities in Wales also mentioned. However, surrounded by the Cardiff Bay Development regeneration area, Butetown locals have been screaming at the tops of their voices for the last twelve years because of the neglect that has brought about the dilapidation and disintegration of the community.

With neglect on such a scale, it should not be surprising that deprivation manifests locally in this way. And it belies any misconception that national monies spent on the regeneration of Cardiff Bay had or has any significant effect on the original communities of Tiger Bay and the Docks which sit at the heart of the development. It is time for concerned members of the community to put their thinking caps on and demand from the authorities better facilities within the community, particularly with reference to the youth, before it is far too late and complete community breakdown occurs.

Although our history has been quite unique as regards its multi-ethnic tolerance, there is a need to examine our own failings as well.

"Where d'you think you're going!" was a common response heard in the old days if you were all dressed up in your best finery on any other day but Sunday. We are not beyond pulling each other down, despite the community's legendary friendliness. And by not supporting each other, we have at times been our own worst enemy.

We have in the past shown a tendency to whinge and moan, complaining among ourselves while failing to address the proper authorities. Is this failing a product of our working-class heritage, or is this a multi-class competitive tradition driven by capitalist culture or, even more sad to say, the universal human condition?

Perhaps, like society at large, we are suffering a community breakdown which has expressed itself universally in the decline of manners and social graces. There is less of the "Please" and "Thank you" these days. And why should Tiger Bay and the Docks be exempt from drug addiction and the resultant social degradation we see virtually everyday or in the media? We are not superhuman. Furthermore, to hear, at a time when our elderly are beginning to feel unsafe, that "Butetown streets are the safest in Cardiff" is a paradox that provides small comfort. Headlining an article in the 17th January 1997 edition of the *South Wales Echo*, this statement should have given a great sense of satisfaction. At last confirmation of what local residents had always known about the area! After all is said and done, folks in Tiger Bay have spent a lifetime defending its reputation, as was stated in *Off Limits*. However, the newspaper article resulted from a meeting which took place on the previous Wednesday at the Mount Stuart Primary School between the police and concerned residents. At that meeting, quite contrary to the promising headline, more and more local people expressed their uneasiness as the situation continues to deteriorate.

In Tiger Bay, the area of particular concern is Angelina Street after dark. As indicated previously, Angelina Street has been ear-marked by the council for demolition in order to rebuild family homes. This is welcome and overdue as the current architecture is rather bleak: the grey brick, prison-like structures compare badly with the original street as laid out during the time of the Second Marquis of Bute. However, as families are moved out and the individual properties are being boarded up problems are increasing. During the day, when ghat is sold, the entire street becomes a market place. At night-time, much to the chagrin of old-time inhabitants, most of the Somali youths, from the community and without, roam the area until at least 5 a.m., congregating near the long-established Somali boarding house and café, creating an all night din and leaving rubbish in their wake.

Thus, on August 30th, 2000, another incident of tragic proportions inevitably occurred. At 2 a.m. trouble exploded when one youth fired a shotgun. What caused this initially seems to be unknown, but, according to rumour, two Somali youths were facing each other on Maria Street in stand-off position. One was aiming a shotgun at the chest of the other, who instantly deflected the weapon as it discharged. Hence the wound to the groin area and not his chest. Hearing the shot explode, Beverly Thomas' young daughter awakened, looked out of her bedroom window and witnessed the incident. Beverly, a long time resident of the maisonettes, contacted the emergency services on hearing the shot ring out. Concerned about the area being secure before sending an ambulance, the dispatcher questioned her about how she knew that it was a shot that she heard.

"If the area wasn't secure *I* wouldn't go out there!" Beverly responded. Her daughter had seen the victim running down Angelina Street from Maria Street. Slamming the phone down, she went to the aid of the stumbling youth. Soon afterwards an armed response team was dispatched. In the meantime, Beverly nursed the twenty-one year old Somali youth in front of Gerald Earnest's house, where he had collapsed. All the while, she kept him conscious as he was drifting into shock. The ambulance arrived at approximately 3:00 a.m., almost forty-five minutes later. Subsequently, the police cordoned off both ends of the street and armed police patrolled the area as the suspect was thought to be hiding out in one of the abandoned properties.

When compared with similar incidents in society at large, the newsworthiness of the two tragic incidents highlighted herein pales into insignificance. And they are not typical of life in the community at all. However, some Somali youths do not appear to have been provided with an understanding or sense of history of the community into which the council has placed them. This has occasionally resulted in the abuse of local white residents who have been made to feel uncomfortable in their home community. On the other hand, other young Somalis have shown greater understanding and have enhanced community relations.

In the autumn of 2000, the Somali Dragons, an amateur football team based in Butetown, became one of the city's most successful clubs, after representing Cardiff in tournaments in Wales and Europe. This success was made possible through financial assistance from Cardiff County Council in the form of an Equality Development Grant, which allowed the team to go to Montecchio Emilia in Italy for the Anti-racism World Championships earlier in the same year. In the council's magazine *Capital Times*, Deputy Mayor Councillor Chris Bettison said, "We are always pleased to support initiatives which encourage community participation and promote fair play. The team has excelled in recent competitions and I am sure they have a bright future."

Hopefully, there will also be a bright future for the community at large, and the Somali community within it, as the new millennium progresses, particularly after Angelina Street is restructured into the kind of street it once was before its 1960s demolition — in a razing which also wrought the destruction of many other streets and byways where cafés and boarding houses created such an exotic and entrancing atmosphere.

Chapter Nine

BOARDING HOUSES & GHOSTS

The posthumous visitation of my maternal relatives, which I mentioned at the beginning of Chapter One, was not the first time in my life that I was profoundly affected by such an event. I had occasion to expound upon my involvement in such matters in *Journey to the Door of the Souls*, chapter two of *Voodoo Detective*, an unpublished manuscript which offers an account of my experiences in Los Angeles, where I lived for the twelve years prior to 1991. The following is an extract which shows how:

> My interest in the occult, or parapsychology as it was becoming known, had always been peripheral, if not non-existent, until I attended a seance with a few friends in Streatham, London toward the end of 1969. This seance was conducted by a medium with a Ouija board. Through this device, which was entirely new to me at that time, I conversed with a pawnshop-keeper who had been murdered in my home town of Cardiff during the mid-fifties. She told of the events of her death; of someone entering her shop and stepping over her body; of the man who killed her; and of an innocent man who had been prosecuted, found guilty and executed. I subsequently wrote about this incident in *The Tiger Bay Story*, identifying Danny Sinclair as the medium. Although unrelated to me, despite her being my grandfather's namesake, she "had never set foot in Cardiff... [yet] ... to my astonishment, under the influence of Lilly Volpert's spirit, she spoke of the day Lilly was killed and named specific locations in Cardiff about which she could not have known."[1] This I found quite extraordinary at the time. What I did not mention in that book was the issue of an alleged letter located in a box under a bed at a certain address in the Grangetown area of Cardiff which would posthumously exonerate the innocent man. At the time of this incident I, my wife, and an American serviceman friend, who had driven us down from London, sat in his car outside that address peering

at the door. However, the fear of the potential embarrassment of having to explain the purpose of our visit outweighed our curiosity and thus we failed to knock the door and eventually drove away, leaving that investigation incomplete.

None the less, considering that the few friends present at the seance, apart from my Cardiff born wife, Anita, had no knowledge of streets or names of people in Cardiff, the revelations from that seance left an odd residual impression which on many occasions caused me to reflect upon the possibility of otherworldly phenomena. However, from then until the incidents described here I had always thought that the "magic" of that moment belonged only to Danny Sinclair and that I myself did not possess such qualities or ability. My understanding of the psychic equality of humanity would later develop from that experience.

While writing *Voodoo Detective* I was also editor of *The Voice of the Tiger*, a quarterly magazine published by Butetown History & Arts Centre. "Boarding Houses & Ghosts" was the title of an essay I published in the Autumn 1995 edition during the time I was a volunteer member of the organisation. As it captures the flavour and atmosphere of the community in the not too distant past, that article is reprinted here with a few slight alterations. Thus, at one time…

Walking down Bute Street you would have passed many cafés, shops and boarding houses like Abdul Satar's (pronounced "Sutter" by locals) and Olive Salaman's Cairo Café.

As you passed by the various cafés, you could see in the windows the many different flags of the countries from which the seamen came and you could smell the many and wonderful aromas of the food stuffs imported from exotic lands. If you turned off Bute Street and entered the back streets of Tiger Bay, you would find many cafés and boarding houses there too.

On North Church Street, for example, there was a sea-men's boarding house run by Mrs. Litchfield, who was related to the Phenis family of Portuguese background. This property and the house next door belonging to the Plaidy family were destroyed in bombing raids during World War II and remained a bomb site until the 1960s demolition. Well before then, at the turn of the century, Evans Best, a ship's carpenter from the island of Barbados, met and married Mrs. Litchfield's daughter May. Thus began the Best family in Tiger Bay which established itself at No. 1 Loudoun Square, the home where Teddy Best, one of their sons, grew up and in his prime, during the 1950s, became a famous boxer.

Abdul Satar, followed by companions, walks along Bute Street with its many cafés and boarding houses as it appeared near to the end of its vibrant days in the 1950s. An onlooker stands nearby on the rain drenched pavement. Satar's well-known seamen's lodging house at 238 was located very near to the corner of South Church Street adjacent to the famous (or some may say "infamous") Rothesay Castle, known locally as the "House of Blazes," and Olive Salaman's Cairo Café. (Photo courtesy of Hulton Getty)

Much further down Bute Street past Tiger Bay was Patrick Street — where Belmont Walk is located today. This street ran all the way to old Alice Street. On its south side, there were large three-storey houses with attics and basements. Like the grand homes in Loudoun Square, they also had steps leading up to the front doors. On the opposite side, the street was divided by Henry Street and the houses were of a more modest nature. At the intersections of these streets was the

Cornish Mount public house.

In the 1950s two of the grand houses located closest to Bute Street, and directly opposite the lane that ran alongside the Cornish Mount, were joined together to form a large seamen's boarding house run by my godmother Lillian Constance Reeves, who once lodged at my parent's home in Frances Street. "Auntie Lil," as she was known to me, was a very distinguished English lady whose upbringing revealed that she had known grander days. Local poet Harry "Shipmate" Cooke remembers seeing her walking with dignified stride along Bute Street in horse-riding jodhpurs. I remember she always smoked cigarettes through a long, elegant cigarette holder. She had come to Tiger Bay long before the Second World War and, in those days, was married to a Panamanian seaman with the colourful nickname of Canal Zone. I believe he died before I used to visit Auntie Lil in her boarding house days. Before then, however, they once had a sweet shop in Maria Street.

"I remember once," said Charlie Waith, "when Canal Zone come out of his shop with his razor after Kenneth Trottman, and Kenneth Trottman wen' in the house and came out with a hatchet. Canal Zone went back in the shop — [and that was the] end of that one." That was one of Charlie Waith's memories of Canal Zone and the exciting street life of the old community.

I am uncertain whether Canal Zone was still alive when Auntie Lil ran the Patrick Street accommodation but in one of the linked houses she catered for Estonian, Norwegian and other Scandanavian seamen, while in the other were West Indians and Africans. Ne'er the twain shall meet! However, the wall

Lillian Constance Reeves whose Patrick Street boarding house provided lodgings to African, West Indian, Estonian and other Baltic and Scandinavian seamen.

(Photo courtesy of the Sinclair family)

separating the basements was knocked down to make a large communal room where the residents did come together with Estonians playing their accordions and the West Indians, their guitars. Also, Auntie Lil had made the two backyards into one large garden, with a rockery and birdbath in the middle, and had planted different kinds of flowers around the edges of the lawn. Those idyllic days and the grand houses of Patrick Street were lost in the demolition of the Docks and Tiger Bay in the 1960s. Also gone was the concern shown by the Cardiff Health Committee for *white women in boarding houses* — which was highlighted in Chapter Two, *That Reputation.*

In Frances Street, just one block up from Loudoun Square, there were two boarding houses. Cardiff street directories indicate that an A. Spathaky ran a Scandanavian boarding house at No. 12

Sapoe Mannay, the African owner of the boarding house on Frances Street. (Photo courtesy of Des Mannay)

and an A. Povanzalli had one at No. 11 in the 1880s. The latter subsequently became an African boarding house run by Sapoe (pronounced "Sipple") Mannay. Apparently, according to Joan Smith who lived next door, a John Davis was the first "coloured man" to live in Frances Street. Joan remembers her "Nana," Mrs. Widegren, telling of the time that neighbours on the street had made a petition to stop him coming to live on the street. Mrs. Widegren, however, whose Swedish husband had died at sea and was buried in Sierra Leone, would not sign, saying that he was "made in God's image the same as everybody else and was entitled to respect and to lead a decent life!" From that day on, he called Joan's grandmother "Mama."

It was in Chapter One of *The Tiger Bay Story*, entitled

"Reminiscences of Streets No More," that I first wrote about my childhood days in the 1940s and 1950s in Frances Street. That street will always hold potent memories for me — like the one that recalls that somewhat grey overcast day when I stood at the front door. But for one lady, I would have been the only soul on the narrow row of terraced houses. With her long hair in a thick braid, she walked slowly down the pavement on the opposite side. She strolled passed the Smiths, the Wellingtons and the Fernandezes, with her baby (little Jannette) in her arms, and a shawl wrapped around her in Welsh fashion to keep her warm and the child protected. As she passed the Dupree's and reached number 4, Mrs. Ali appeared at her front door remonstrating and shouting at the lady. I was too young then to now recall the origin of this disturbance, but it may have been something to do with walking on the street on a cold day with a young baby or some such thing. In any event, it seemed to have an adverse affect on the lady. Whatever it was, Iris turned and cried out:

"Mind your own business! What's it to do with you!"

Suddenly the lady fell to the ground in tears. As she struck the pavement I ran inside to raise the alarm. Alas, this memory begins to fade into mist but I remember opening the living room door and yelling:

"Mam, a lady just fell down in the street."

A fews days later, I heard Iris Williams of No. 2 was dead. It was about the same time that I found myself puzzled by Mrs Duallah, a black lady from Ireland, who came to live in what had been Sapoe Mannay's African boarding house. Years later, her son Moses Hassan told me his grandfather was a Brazilian seaman who, after docking in Belfast, fell in love with the landlady of the boarding house that he stayed in there. And soon Moses' mother Prudence was born. She grew up in Belfast and years later she in turn fell in love with a Mr. Hassan, a Somali seaman who had also docked there. However, he had already made his home in Tiger Bay. Soon she would arrive in Wales to live there for the rest of her life.

After arriving in Tiger Bay, the family settled at No. 1 Peel Street in an Arab boarding house owned by Egyptian seaman Said Mohammed. This establishment was situated at the corner of Gladstone Street, the cobblestoned lane which led up to the side of St Mary's church on South Church Street. In that house Moses was born. Subsequently, Prudence remarried Mohamed Duallah Mohamed, who had been a leader of the Somali Youth League and a member of the Communist Party since the early 1920s. Soon other sons were born to them, includ-

Said Mohammed's boarding house at No 1 Peel Street and the corner of Gladstone Street appears in the rear between Betty Campbell and the author. This photograph, taken in 1958, also shows the rear wall of the South Church Street Board School playground. (Photo courtesy of the Sinclair family)

ing Ibrahim — known to everyone as Brian. Eventually, the Duallahs moved to the African boarding house in Frances Street, where I first came to know them. By that time, the Duallahs had become the sole occupants.

Now it just so happened that Mr. Mohammed's Arab boarding house on Peel Street, where they first stayed, was haunted — as were so many other homes in Tiger Bay in those days, according to local folklore. Various apparitions made their appearance at that rather interesting boarding house for Arab, Egyptian and other African seamen. This was one of those big old houses that were common in Tiger Bay then. At the top of this three storey house was a large room that could hold twenty-five beds. There was no carpet on the stairs that led to that big room but Kitty Said, Mr. Mohammed's wife, used to scrub those wooden stairs until they were almost white.

One day, my aunt Helen Sinclair went to stay there. Farida, Mr. Mohammed's daughter, warned Helen that the house was haunted. However, Helen, it seems, took that warning with a grain of salt and decided to stay anyway.

As it was, one night when Helen was about to retire, she ran in fright from her room after seeing a man sitting there. Trying to wake Farida she shouted, "There's a man in my room!"

"I told you," said Farida rather matter of factly, "It's him!" And she went promptly back to sleep.

"I warned you. I told you the house is haunted by an old Somali seaman. He always goes to the back room where you slept!" said Farida the following day in response to Helen's nocturnal alarm.

In Tiger Bay, there were many Arab boarding houses in those days like Abdul Satar's on Bute Street. The impeccably dressed Yusef Shurra, a seaman friend of Mr Mohammed, lived in one on Nelson Street not too far away. This is the same street where, years before, Jim Nurse had his little altercation with a policeman, as was mentioned

Helen Sinclair with daughter Anne-Marie in pushchair and author outside St Mary the Virgin Church in 1958. Taken a year or so after Aunt Helen had stayed at the haunted boarding house on Peel Street.
(Photo courtesy of the Sinclair family)

in Chapter Three. It was also the home of Victor Parker, Tiger Bay's celebrated guitar player and singer. On this same street lived another natural musician who could play the piano without effort and without ever learning to read a note. She was Phyllis Jones, who would eventually marry Isaac Freeman, an African seaman, and raise a family in Loudoun Square. (Incidentally, Mr Freeman stood his ground and refused to leave during the 1960s demolition, causing his home on the west side of Loudoun Square to be the last one standing amidst the rubble of a desolate landscape. The effects of that time on others will be explored in the following chapter.) In those days, when Victor Parker was a young man, spiritualism was in vogue. It must have been a popular pastime: for example, people still recall that Gilbey Freeman's mother was one

Two musicians from Tiger Bay: Victor Parker with guitar and singer Benny Mohammed, known in the entertainment world as Sy Scott, in white jacket. Circa 1970.
(Photo courtesy of Stella Hersi)

who had the "gift." She was also my godmother and, of course, the Phyllis Jones already mentioned. At the time, she lived with her sister, Gwyneth, next door to the Hutchins. From the outside,

Gilbey Freeman (2nd from right), whose mother had the "gift", on board ship with local and foreign seamen. Circa late 1940s.
(Photo courtesy of BHAC)

their house looked like all the terraced houses on the street but, at some time in the past, it must have been a pub or some such, because in the back was a very large room like a hall. It was in that room that seances were conducted with large groups attending.

Mr. Mohammed's boarding house on Peel Street was of great interest because more than one ethereal visitor continued to make its appearance up to the time compulsory purchase was placed on the property shortly before the demolition of old Tiger Bay in the 1960s. By this time, Mr. Mohammed was ill and failing and it was his custom to bang his walking stick on the floor when he wanted his wife Kitty to make him his favourite beverage and bring it up to him. One night as Kitty was climbing up the stairs, hot drink in hand, a dark gentleman in a trilby hat and overcoat stood to one side to let her pass.

The traditional Middle Eastern style mosque on Peel Street shortly before its demolition and replacment by the less traditional and modern structure that stands on the same site today.
(Photo courtesy of BHAC)

"That Yusef Shurra didn't speak to me when I passed him on the stairs. What's the matter with him?" she said, as she put the coffee down.

"What are you bringing me coffee for?" responded Mr. Mohammed.

"You knocked the floor!" said Kitty.

"No I didn't!" said he, "and Yusef Shurra hasn't been here to visit me either!"

"He's out there now!" Kitty protested. But as she opened the door to see him, the light from the street lamp on Gladstone Street shone onto the door and in that instant the man in the trilby hat and overcoat vaporised into thin air before her eyes.

In much the same way, the Mosque which once graced Peel Street, the first ever to be built in Britain for the Moslem community, has also vanished into the mist. However, unlike Peel Street itself, it has been replaced — although by a less appealing modern version.

Like the boarding houses and ghosts, so much of the character and mystique of Tiger Bay and the Docks has disappeared into the mists of time. The 1960s demolition has seen to that. With few exceptions, the open doors of yesteryear are bolted shut. No one walks into your house at New Year to poke the fire and bring good luck to the household. Karaoki in the few remaining pubs has replaced the piano that locals sang around. It has also replaced the roving troubadours who played mandolin, guitar, bottle or whatever to make a joyous sound and warm the hearts of all at Christmas time. No more are distinct aromas to be inhaled from the shops on Bute Street and the back kitchens of the seamen's boarding houses which once dotted the community.

Chapter Ten

THE FIRST BLOW - WHAT THE DEMOLITION DID

"Butetown, half-forgotten in the decline of the docks, could play a crucial role in the Buchanan Plan for Cardiff," proferred an encouraging *Western Mail* article published in the 27 August 1968 edition. Written by George Yeoman, lecturer in town planning at the University of Wales Institute of Science and Technology, and previously referred to in Chapter Three, this unfulfilled ambition appeared at a time when much of the community looked like a devastated wasteland as the 1960s redevelopment was taking shape. The tower blocks began to be erected in the centre of the Loudoun Square park and the original architecture of the area, inspired by the Second Marquis of Bute, came under threat as the bulldozers and wrecking balls began their course of destruction at the north end of the community displacing its Greek and Cypriot residents as these monstrous machines moved south. Experienced as an attack by the council upon the residents newly brought under its jurisdiction, this first strike at old Tiger Bay was discussed in detail in Chapter Seven, "Nuclear Bomb On Tiger Bay" in *The Tiger Bay Story*. As Yeoman outlined in his article, the Buchanan Plan, which followed in the wake of that first destabilisation of the community, was designed to boost commerce and industry in Cardiff. Yeoman suggested also that this plan include the revitalization of the decaying business sector in Mount Stuart Square and bring further office development into South Cardiff. Although this Plan never came to fruition, it was a precursor to the eventual transformation of the area into Cardiff Bay. At that time Yeoman believed that "while enough of its economy remains as a nucleus for growth," Butetown's revival was imperative and went on to say that "dominated by its past, this [the Plan] can be the springboard for its future." Of

148

course the road net-
work described in
the Plan, which
would have rein-
forced the barriers
around Butetown,
further segregating it
from the city, did not
re-emerge after the
plan was abandoned.
As for the "crucial

Mount Stuart Square during its vibrant heyday. (Photo courtesy of BHAC)

role" Butetown could play in the resurrection of enterprise in
Cardiff, that, too, faded into the mist, as it remained a Cardiff
City Council housing estate outside the jurisdiction of the
Cardiff Bay Development Corporation which came into existence much later in 1987. By that time, community members
had already undergone a quite traumatic upheaval, both physi-
cally and spiritually.

"And very soon it will be our turn to go — my husband
and I," begins the first line of *So Sinks Tiger Bay*, an unpublished memoir of life-long resident Beatrice Sinclair. Saddened by the break up of the community she loved, my
mother's story continues:

> … we are back where we started. Our daughter Leslie having
> married and given us three lovely grandchildren, Stephen,
> Vanessa and baby Melanie. Our youngest son Neil having
> gone to America. We leave this home which witnessed our
> sorrow at the loss of our beloved sons Leonard and Ronald.
> Losing Leonard at not quite two was bad but Ronald at sixteen
> years — that nearly *did for us* but you have to go on somehow.
> I can see now from my window the 15 storey flats that are now
> complete. It gives me a queer feeling to realise soon I'll be able
> to see from a new window the bulldozer destroying my old
> home of so many memories. It seemed that for a long time
> people and things stayed the same in Tiger Bay. We were like

a village community. But when the news of new houses being built came, people from other places seemed to arrive over-night. Now Tiger Bay is called Butetown and … the families have moved out …

From my window I have been able to see the beginning of the end of Tiger Bay. Families I have known for years moving from the old to the new. Some not too happily, being … so young and knowing all mod cons does not make up for old known homes and their memories — sad and happy — but known to them.

Although saddened by the demolition, Beatrice, the daughter of a West Indian seafarer and a Lancashire-born mother, was fortunate that she was still going to remain in the same geographical location staked out by the residents of old Tiger Bay. Many others departed from the community forever. Some believed in the promise that they would return, once additional housing had been rebuilt. But moving, as we all know, is not always easy after settling down. Thus some, like the late jazz singer Millie Houter née Grant, did not return until the early 1990s. However, while the hunt to rout the Tiger progressed, many were adamant they were not going to leave at all — as happened in the case of Olwen Watkins née Blackman.

On her way home from shopping in town, Olwen could not believe the audacity of what she assumed to be a *down-and-out* sitting on the steps of her family's Loudoun Square town house.

"Er! What 'you doing there!" she said quite indignantly.

"You've gotta get out!" said he.

"What d'you mean. Get off my doorstep!" she shouted as she prodded him.

"I'm the man who's going to knock your house down!" he fatally exclaimed.

As the fate of the already-demolished houses that surrounded her drew closer to her own, the impact of this statement struck at the foundation of Olwen's soul. Internally she quaked with tears at the realisation of what the man had said.

"Where d'you wanna go?" the man inquired.

"I'm not going anywhere," she responded.

"What about Llanrummney or Ely, then," he went on.

"I told you, I'm not going! she retorted emphatically.

"But you've got to!"

"I don't have to *got to* anything," she said. "I'm not a cow or a cat. You can't tell me I've got to get out!" she remonstrated in vain.

She knew she was fighting a losing battle, but she was not going to move out of the only home she knew. The only place she knew where she was accepted. The place of her birth.

Olwen on a tricycle being helped by Rachel ("Auntie Ray") Farrah and watched over by her mother Lydia Blackman in the late 1930s. Notice the railings which were removed during the Second World War and the fountain which was still the main feature in the centre of the park then. (Photo courtesy of Olwen Watkins)

"I was born on the 23rd October 1935 — four years before the war broke out," an account of Olwen's life begins.

Marika Sherwood, a researcher for the Association for the Study of African, Caribbean and Asian Culture and History in Britain, encouraged her to tell her story, as it exemplified the multi-ethnic mixture found in so many families born into the Tiger Bay mileux. With her permission, extracts from her narrative *Black and Welsh,* which tell of a time when the vital force and power of the Tiger was at its height, are reproduced here. They also explain why many of Cardiff's docklands old-time residents still pine for former days and how deeply felt is the wound that left a beaten and still endangered Tiger.

"I was born into a multi-racial, multi-religious community, thank God," Olwen's account begins. She goes on to say:

> Over time it evolved into a tight-knit neighbourhood with its own home grown culture, the main tenet of which was tolerance.
>
> Everyone, no matter from where they came, could find a home and friendship in Butetown. There were many immigrants around the turn of the century, when maps of the world glowed with the bright pink splashes telling the story of British conquest and colonisation. And so people arrived — mainly men who were coming to what was now their motherland, where hopefully the living would be easy; or easier and better paid than at home. Many of those who came to settle in Butetown, as our area was called, came from those pink splashes on the map — from India, Malaysia, the British West Indies, China, Arabia, Africa. There were a few Americans and even the man who was believed to be the *only* Native American in Wales. Basque steel workers came to work in that industry at Dowlais in the Welsh valleys. Their families followed and soon there was a substantial Spanish/Basque community here...
>
> We always had a large Muslim community, consisting of Arabs, Somalis, Egyptians, Sudanese, West Africans and Malays. Not all the immigrants were British subjects. There were Greeks, Cypriot and Turkish communities as well as Norwegian, Danish, Swedish and Estonian....

Loudoun Square, where I grew up, is named after a Bute estate in Scotland. When my mother was a child, about seventy years ago (i.e. circa 1920s), the square was very sedate and quiet, almost exhorting interlopers to walk on tip-toe. This was where the moneyed people lived. But as their fortunes grew, they moved further and further out into the suburbs, building even grander houses for themselves. And so these lovely houses in this impeccable square became the homes of those who worked in and around the docks. My family moved into Loudoun Square from Angelina Street…

I always thank God for being born in Butetown and for making me a hybrid. I have imbibed an alternative education by sitting at the knees of my African uncles: one a Portuguese African, the other a Liberian African. They were the husbands of two of my mother's sisters. A third, Aunt Sarah, 'went on the stage' and trod the boards around a good part of the world. She married a Romanian.

My great-grandmother was the one who sowed the seeds of the 'international brigade' that our family was to become. She emigrated from the Republic of Ireland to Liverpool in the 19th century. She made her living there by running a boarding house for seamen. She was a staunch Catholic and disappointed neither parent, priest nor Pope as she married another Catholic. He was Sidro Aguillos, a Filipino seaman from the island of Ilo Ilo, where the Catholic faith had been introduced by the Spanish colonisers. Their daughter Annie, my grandmother, also married a seaman. He had arrived in Britain via Haiti from somewhere else in the West Indies. They had four children who were all given Biblical or classical names. They were Sarah Hortensia, Sylvia, Minerva, and the boy Francis.

My grandmother married a second time. I have no idea what happened to her first husband. Sarah, my only living aunt, will be a hundred years old this year (c. 1996) but cannot tell me any family stories as she is suffering from the ravages of senile decay. Annie's second husband was Henry Hopkins, a ship's mate from Cat Key in the Bahamas. They had a daughter, Lydia, my mother.

Mother married Henry Edward George Mafeking Blackman, who was of English/Welsh origin. His last name comes from the fact that at the time of his birth his father was fighting in the Boer War and was caught up in the siege of Mafeking. My father was born during the relief of that siege — hence the name.

My father had a sister, Aunty Kate, who was great fun. She married three times, each time an African seaman. There was no issue from the first marriage; three from the second and two from the third. Although she was a white woman, she could dance like an African. She was always happy. [She had six] children... Judy became a singer performing with the top radio bands in the 1940s. Mac was a very quiet person. He went to sea as soon as he was old enough. Grace and Charles were the last two Johnson offspring. Later, from Aunty Kate's third marriage came Betty and Henry Kingston, whose father did not see them into maturity.

My family is just one example of the many mixed-race families within the Butetown community. The culture that guided our mode of life had evolved over a period of more than a hundred years. The basis, the beginning of it, was the system of overlapping extended families which provided us with a free welfare system. There were always baby-sitters, carers, midwives and even people who could lay out the dead. As a community we had to learn how to survive on our own. Historically we have been berated and denigrated by the population which has become known as the 'host' nation. These are people who thrive on mythology and false stereotypes, which provide them with a feeling of superiority. They cling to the bawdy days which probably never existed, during Cardiff's boom-time, when men were recruited to build the docks. There were no leisure activities except drinking, eating and sleeping. Boom-towns always have their camp followers, and there was probably prostitution but that was in the 1800s. It is said that prostitution is a trade as old as time. Butetown is thought by some to be the most iniquitous place in Great Britain. But prostitution can be found everywhere, and every city has its fringe. I always imagined Cardiff's building boom of the 1840s to be similar to the gold rush in California which was essentially a male adventure. Here, too, that male-dominated society was soon to see the arrival of those females seeking a route to riches from the poverty of their times.

As we have seen in recent times, those who have will still seek to augment their bank balances through fair means and foul, and quite often at the expense of someone of lesser means.

I would not mind the stereotyped way the Outsiders have formed their perception of us, as long as they do no more to us than they already have.

Loudoun Square Park, the centre of community life in Tiger Bay as it was in the mid 1950s, awaits the demise of its former glorious days as the 1960s demolition approaches.
(Photo courtesy of Olwen Watkins)

As Cardiff grew and eventually became a city and then the capital of Wales, the City Fathers felt that this community could only damage Cardiff's integrity ... and without real knowledge of how it really was, they thought of a way to rid themselves of what was a blot on the city. They have replaced it with a council estate and dispersed as many of the remnants of long-time families as they could to other parts of the city. I, for one, refused to move, opting to move into a two bed apartment on the 5th floor of a fifteen storey block of flats, which they planted right in the middle of Loudoun Square, which had been a lovely park with a ring of trees inside the perimeter stone wall. No one can convince me that this was not a blow to the integrity of our community, which policed itself and worked very well for many a year without the need for outside agencies. Although the place has changed, not for the better I might add, it will be a long time before it can become the cohesive entity it once was. I will always mourn the place I grew up in. It will never be the same. I expect to end my days here. But who knows eh? …

Olwen's personal interpretation of the last days of the old community exposes the extent of the damage done to its social fabric but, like a reflection in an endless hall of mirrors where an image catapults itself into infinity, the loss of the old caring ways is, of course, an experience many working-class communities in Great Britain shared during the post-war era.

Although we share this loss with other communities throughout the nation, our council estate is unique in that it was foisted onto an already-existing, ancient, multi-generational community. The BBC television producer Michael Bogdanov, who recreated several Shakespearean dramas in council estate settings, observed this very point when his company researched our community a few years ago in order to film *The Tempest in Butetown*.

Although his attempt to popularise Shakespeare in this manner confused many, Bogdanov's observations elicited a much truer perception of the nature of Tiger Bay life than did the soap opera *Tiger Bay*, produced by BBC Wales in the late 1990s. An opportunity was lost to bring to the wider United Kingdom television audience a successful series similar to *EastEnders* or *Brookside* — tinged with a Welsh flavour. The influence of Welsh culture on aspects of Tiger Bay life was distorted when not completely overlooked. South Wales valleys' culture, accent and nuances were superimposed onto an Afro-Celtic and multi-ethnic urban culture. The reality of local life near the sea was misrepresented.

Many of the old structures, including our home on Frances Street, still remain in view here as the old ways of Tiger Bay draw to a close while the tower blocks rise in the heart of our community during the early 1960s.
(Photo courtesy of BHAC)

The BBC's failure to capture a Tiger Bay in fiction that would have had popular appeal is not surprising. In its understanding of the true nature of life in the community, which should have formed the backdrop to this fiction, it has been grossly misrepresented and unduly influenced by the negative mythology, explored earlier in *That Reputation*.

Equally cataclysmic as Othello's betrayal, the misplaced attempt at modernity represented by the lacklustre edifices of the Butetown council estate that replaced the more human dimensions of the original well-crafted architecture casts a disheartening shadow over the old multi-ethnic community of Tiger Bay, making its loss singular and all the more poignant.

Chapter Eleven

DEDICATION AND BETRAYAL

Despite the vicissitudes of two world wars, the aforegoing has shown that the community of Tiger Bay and the Docks has fended for itself quite effectively. However the 1960s demolition, which struck the initial blow to its apparent self-sufficiency, and the social decline and physical dereliction the community continued to undergo as a stepchild of the 1990s regeneration, has weakened its resolve.

As circumstances dictate today, the disappearance of venues for social activity within the *problem estate* has deprived mature young people in our community of a place to unleash their energies constructively and no doubt contributed to the crime wave which crested in the Bay in 1994. Who is to blame? What is there for young people to do in today's Butetown? They are too old for Youth Centres, such as exist, too young to receive Income Support and, despite all promises, unemployed. How does today's situation compare with the community of yesterday?

At the beginning of the twenty-first century we have come to accept the whole of Britain as a multicultural state. This aspect of life is old hat in Tiger Bay. Just as New York's Ellis Island filtered European immigrants into the United States, the vast majority of ethnic minorities who came to Wales prior to and during the first half of the 20th century passed through Tiger Bay. (The fact that Newport and Thompson Street, that other Tiger Bay in Barry Docks, which formed strong ties with our community, can also lay claim to forming small multi-ethnic nuclei is not overlooked.)

Encouragingly, the last decades of the twentieth century saw multi-ethnic politics rise to a prominent level and racial equality laws enacted, including the establishment of the offices of the Commission for Racial Equality across the entire United Kingdom. In addition to the CRE, Cardiff also has the offices of Race Equality First, Cadmad, Awema and

A group of Arab and African seamen who formed part of that other "Tiger Bay" in Barry Docks. Taken in the 1940s near Eleanor Farrah's boarding house on old Thompson Street before it too was deprived of its architectural charm and like the old streets of Tiger Bay demolished.
(Photo courtesy of BHAC)

Multicultural Crossroads, among others, whose stated agenda is the improvement of conditions for ethnic minorities throughout Wales. But what about Tiger Bay, the original homeland of multiculturalism in Wales? How are they helping? What are they not doing? Are they making matters worse? Do they care? Are they using us? Does it matter to us?

In *The Tiger's Youth*, chapter nine of *The Tiger Bay Story*, I referred to "various ... ex-colonial types used to 'dealing' with colonial subjects ... [who were] commissioned to work in Tiger Bay as if it was actually a colony within Europe. In some quarters this attitude continues and needs to be addressed."

The strongest reaction to the ineffectiveness of the Commission for Racial Equality comes from the inhabitants of the original, multi-ethnic community of Tiger Bay and the Docks. At the beginning of this new millennium, people in the community perceive themselves as more colonised by outside groups than ever. Thus, in an effort to appeal to the grassroots, the CRE saw the necessity for revamping its image in South Wales in October 2000. However, in a Welsh television newsbroadcast of 10th October, the community's perception of the CRE as elitist and distant from its needs was expressed by local activist Keith Murrell of NewEmploy Wales. Indeed, some interviewees in the same broadcast were unaware of the CRE's existence. Some in the community, however, do recognise the role the CRE plays in facilitating other organisations which interface with it.

Unfortunately, the same community perception is shared with regard to such related institutions as Race Equality First. Despite the resources available, the experience of many is that this organisation does not address their needs: this perception has to be effectively addressed. Situated outside the community, its members do not sufficiently penetrate the community and therefore do not really know what the needs are. As Chapter Six illustrated, racial discrimination in employment is not new to the residents of Tiger Bay. The community has undergone an economic depression whose historical dimensions are apparently undetected by such groups. Prior to the existence of such well funded organisations as the CRE and Race Equality First, men and women in the community were employed in the docks as seamen or factory and dock workers. There was always some form of employment available "locally." However, those who wished to find employment above the bridge often experienced racial discrimination.

Patti Flynn (née Young), who had ambitions to be a shop clerk in the retail industry, having seen many signs in the shop windows for *help wanted*, is one who has such memories. In the late 1940s, having recently left school with high scholastic achievement, Patti went to the Labour Exchange on Westgate Street seeking a job opportunity. She and another friend would sit all afternoon at the Exchange watching other Cardiff girls leave the premises on their way to interviews only to be told at the end of the day:

"Sorry, but there are no jobs for you today!"

After a few weeks of such treatment, Patti wandered St Mary Street and the other major shopping streets of town looking for signs for work in their windows. Polite, timid inquiries were made, but she was always just a little too late for the advertised job.

Patti Flynn centred amongst family and friends at an outing in Cardiff Castle grounds in the mid 1950s. (Photo courtesy of the Sinclair family)

Persistently rejected by management in the uptown shops, strategy and boldness were required when Patti noticed a sign still in a shop window a week after she had been blatantly declined employment. Enraged but determined, she finally spoke out:

"Tell me, does this shop employ *coloured* people or not? You see, I don't want to waste my time," she said after having asked a shop assistant to fetch the manager.

"Come into the office," said the startled man who, unused to being directly confronted in such a manner, beckoned Patti through.

"Well, we have never hired one before and I'm not sure how our customers will take to it," he told her. "But if you want,

I'll give you a week's try, to see how things go."

Patti jumped at the opportunity. Being a Docks girl with a vivacious, outgoing personality helped her win over the customers who were more than familiar with the nuances and humour of this native-born Welsh girl, albeit one with an attractive caramel-brown face. In her small but courageous way Patti helped to pioneer the breaking down of a barrier that would remain erect for far too many years after that time. Patti Young would go on to become Patti Flynn, the cabaret artiste who is still going strong on the Continent today. In recent times, Patti has found permanent fame, as the Cardiff Bay Art Trust has carved her name into the pavement in Bute Street. Along with George Glossop, the guitarist who taught Victor Parker, their names can be found together, near the entrance to Letton ("Tom-the-Fish") Way.

With the prospect of finding work on the docks, only the most ardent persisted in their efforts to break through uptown discrimination in an effort to improve their circumstances. However, after the 1950s, with the accelerated decline in shipping and the closure of many factories and businesses which depended upon and supported the docks, unemployment became a chronic issue for the community — as conditions remained unchanged above the bridge.

In the past, there were no well-resourced organisations such as there are today to help young people achieve, but there were individuals like Jim Nurse, Aaron Mossell, Mohamed Duallah Mohamed, Alan Shepherd, Flori Fernandez, Rene Philips, Martin Caines, and Chalkie White, MBE. They belonged to such former groups as *The Coloured Brotherhood*, the *Sons of Africa*, the *Somali Youth League*, the *Colonial Club* and the *Quakers*, who did their best to inspire them. While members of the former groups lived in and formed an integral part of the community, members of today's organisations tend to be external and are regarded as being out of touch with community needs.

An outsider who did take a great interest in the youth of Tiger Bay was Iorwerth John, a member of the Quaker movement. Mr John, who came to live in the community during the second World War and started the Play Centre on Bute Street (which, by the time of my youth, had become the Neptune Club run by Donald Andrews), reconnected with the community during the mid 1990s.

"[A]t 80 years of age and having lived in six dwellings since leaving Tiger Bay, I have gone through a process of disposing of papers, notes and other such documents at the various stages. I have little else left but my memory and that, as one would expect, is deteriorating," said Mr John in correspondence with researcher Marika Sherwood.

Fortunately, Iorwerth John's memory is still vivid enough to intimately remember social activists like Alan Shepherd, whom he affectionately refers to as "Shep," and Paul Robeson's uncle-in-law Aaron Mossell, an African American who lodged with the Jason family on the west side of Loudoun Square.

According to Iorwerth John, Aaron Mossell attended the Pacific Service Unit, which came together in Cardiff about 1940, and also the old Adult School — along with Loudoun Square resident Edward Bovell, a Barbadian seaman, "a delightful old man known to everyone in the Docks as Uncle Ned."

Aaron Mossell had been a lawyer in Philadelphia before travelling to South Africa prior to arriving in Wales. At his lodgings in Loudoun Square he kept a large collection of books on social struggle and although he took a great interest in political issues, John does not recall him or Uncle Ned as Party political creatures: they "talked of other things."

These two and Alan Shephard were my closest friends in Tiger Bay. Although Shep was a communist, and I frequently went to have a chat with him in his home, we never talked party politics. We developed a great respect for one another. He knew I was a Christian and he thought a great deal of the Quakers. We would talk current affairs, the progress of the war, conditions in the docks and his own family affairs — his two boys (Bobby and Alan) came to our children's club.

As a Unit our concern was, of course with people, their families and their social conditions. When living in the Meeting House we had a first aid post there and trained in first-aid and home nursing, but when (air) raids subsided we turned to the Docks and went to live there.

According to John two Quakers named Rowntree and Gilbert founded a settlement in the valleys to help unemployed miners and their families during the times of the Depression. Apparently, after other Quakers had introduced him to the Maes-yr-Haf Settlement at Trealaw, Aaron Mossell met George Young, a friend of Iorwerth John, at one of the monthly meetings in the Rhondda, and inspired him to form the *South Wales Association for the Welfare of Coloured People* in order to combat colour prejudice. John's interesting memoirs indicate that he also took a principle interest in the Association:

When we moved to live in Bute Street, George asked me to take over the Association. Aaron and Uncle Ned were members and George used to hold a special meeting for worship from time to time in the Meeting House on a weekday evening to which he would invite people from Tiger Bay. Aaron and Ned would always be there. Others attending, perhaps half a dozen, were nearly all Africans or West Indian and in all probability attached to the Methodist Church in Loudoun Square.

Evidently well respected among the men of Tiger Bay, John speaks highly of his close friendship with Alan Shepherd who "was in many ways very independent — it used to be said, by way of a joke I believe, that he was turned out of the Communist group because he was too far left." Intriguingly John's account throws light on the community's interest in anti-colonial politics by describing the time when Alan Shepherd played host to an African, who was to take an influential role in the liberation of colonial Africa:

> One occasion which still stands out in my memory was when, in the early 1940s, Shep came around to invite me to a meeting with Jomo Kenyata. He took me to a lane parallel to Bute Street where there was a large wooden shed at the back of one of the houses.

(The lane John refers to was Bute Lane, which extended from Gladstone Street at its north end all the way down to Patrick Street. John's description of a wooden shed on the lane leads me to believe that it was the same place where West Indian Roy Jenkins later kept a workshop — at the corner of Bute Lane and North Loudoun Place. As Roy also used the upstairs as a clubhouse in my youth, it was a place I and other local children often frequented. In particular, I remember playing above that workshop with Keith Best, Brian Bishop and Anthony Evora, although when we played at the clubhouse, we had no idea that the future liberator of Kenya had once been there.) John's description goes on to say that in:

> a workshop on the ground floor there was a wooden stairway to an upper room. When we reached the room, although I was aware of the presence of a few persons I could see nobody. Gradually, in the candle light, about eight black faces began to materialize and I realized that mine was the only white face they were looking at. I could then see Kenyata's huge form and the flashy rings on his fingers. It dawned on me that Shep was paying a compliment to my honesty and wanted me to experience this privilege. Alas, I can find no notes of the procedure. In any case, I would never have dreamed of taking notes at the

time, even if I would have seen to do so. All I can say is that
Kenyata was travelling around wherever he had the opportunity to speak with African people about his visions of a Pan
Africa. Shep, of course, was swept up by this. I think he had
faith that if only this could be achieved the African peoples
would set up a new kind of society. When freedom came to the
African countries one after another I believe Shep must have
suffered a great disillusionment. My short-term in Ghana
showed me how people in the developing African countries
were determined to obtain for themselves the privileges and
material rewards that they had seen the British enjoying. The
Ghanaians were a friendly, cheerful people but in two very
divided groups. This was far from what Shep had visualized.

John also remembered other local Arab, Somali, Maltese, West Indian and African groups which had been formed
largely to establish an ethnic or national identity rather than for
political reasons. The West Indians and Africans tended to be
Christian, many of them attending the Methodist Church. "The
Arabs, of course, were fairly faithful to Islam" and, John
recalls, "generally independent as the Colonial Office had built
a mosque for them."

As a seaport community with sailors from the four
quarters of the world, it was inevitable that these men would
take native-born women for wives. This was obvious to Iorwerth
John who, reflecting on this circumstance, said:

Mostly, the men of other races had married white women and
settled down to bring up families. However, Lydia, the lady
who used to clean the children's Play Centre, was the only
Afro woman I knew who was married to a white Englishman,
Harry Blackman. Their daughter (Olwen) was the first person
to go to Teacher Training College. Two of the boys from our
Play Centre became fairly well known boxers: Joe Erskine and
Phil Edwards and another became a professional rugby player:
Billy Boston.

Like Iorwerth John, another temporary visitor to the community during the 1940s was African American anthropologist St Clair Drake who returned to America to teach at Roosevelt University in Chicago and then later at Stanford University (where he trained Glenn Jordan, Director of Butetown History & Arts Centre). Impressed by the harmonious multi-ethnic mix of Tiger Bay, his research on our community would have a later impact, as will be discussed later.

Although not common knowledge, it is well documented that there were many black lawyers in Britain during the late Victorian and early Edwardian eras. Primarily located in London, metropolitan capital of the British colonial world, these men from Africa or of African or Caribbean descent made their mark in legal history. Among them were men like Isaac Pixley Seme, who was called to the bar in 1910, having previously "enrolled at Jesus College, Oxford."[1] For Wales, this sort of achievement was not to arrive until after the Second World War when, inspired by the efforts of some of the aforementioned community activists, Docks Boy Manuel Delgado, known to everyone in the community as Lella, became a solicitor and Wales' first black councillor.

Part of the local Cape Verdian community, Manuel Delgado was one of seven children raised in Mount Stuart Square prior to the 1960s demolition — which saw the square, which still contains the magnificent Coal Exchange building, transformed from a residential area exclusively into a business sector. Having won a scholarship to Howard Garden High School, he eventually graduated in law from Bristol University.

"He was a small boy who used to help me," wrote Lord Callaghan, who recalled in a letter that, at a later date, Manuel "went to Barry and became a solicitor."

Following his untimely death, the *South Wales Echo* of 17 January 1996 said:

Mr Delgado became the first coloured magistrate in Cardiff in 1969 and chairman of the Race Relations Board's conciliation committee for Wales and the West three years later.

Ten years ago he was appointed chairman of the Industrial Tribunal in Birmingham and moved to Warwickshire where he died of a heart attack at home last Thursday.

Although his funeral service was held at St Teilo's Roman Catholic Church in Whitchurch, the after-funeral reception held in his honour took place in the Butetown Community Centre, where local people came to show their respect in typical, effusive Tiger Bay fashion.

Before the council-instituted Butetown Community Centre there was a home grown centre, the George Cross, that had a definite impact on the community and inspired many young people to take a constructive path in life. After the departure of much of Tiger Bay's Maltese community in the 1950s, many recall the dedication shown by Stewart Martin Caines, Alan Shepherd and Vivian "Chalkie" White, MBE when they established the George Cross, which had previously served the needs of the Maltese community, as the community centre of the day.

"Table tennis up looong time ago," Mr Caines often said in his inimitable African accent, as David Bourne, Gerald Adullahi and many others recall. This phrase would be heard when he decided youngsters had had their money's worth playing the game. Also at the George Cross were The Saints, an all girls' netball and baseball team, which included among others the late Iris John, Betty Neil and Olwen Blackman.

Brian "Ibrahim" Ahmed recalls how, as a lad, he paid sixpence to play in the snooker room. Once inside, he would open the window and let the other Bay Boys in for free! While another local resident recalls Mr Shepherd and Chalkie White being quite upset when they realised they were running an unofficial babysitting service. Some mothers willingly gave their young children a penny so they could leave them at the

George Cross watching the telly while the mums got a worthy break!

However, games were not the only entertainment these local men provided. Mrs Lesley Clarke, while carrying her first child Stephen, remembers learning to appreciate opera in one of the rooms at the centre. I remember paying a penny to go in one room and watch television, which few people had in the 1950s. There I saw for the first time the BBC children's roundabout with Bill & Ben, the Flowerpot Men, Andy Pandy, Muffin the Mule and the Mumblies.

These facilities helped a whole generation of youth and turned their juvenile lust for adventure away from dangerous and criminal activity. Although small, the George Cross offered classes in dress-making, needlework, languages, music appreciation, games, and more. In addition, dances were also held in the George Cross that sometimes rivalled those at Mr French's Annexe further down Bute Street. The Sons of Africa also held their political meetings there.

Renowned dancer Laura Savage jitterbugging away with Rupert Martinez at the Friday Hop that used to take place at old St Mary's School until the late 1950s. Like many others, Laura learned to jive at the Colonial Centre and was often seen dancing at the George Cross and Frenchie's Annex.
(Photo courtesy of Hulton Getty)

In those days, Stewart Martin Caines was a notable character in the streets of Tiger Bay. He resided in lodgings at the home of fellow African, John Davids, a Liberian seaman, near Gunderson's Fish & Chip Shop and Berlin's Milk

Bar, a Somali-owned café in Sophia Street. Mr Caines, although born in Mozambique, Africa, had been educated in British Guyana in South America before coming to Tiger Bay. Some local residents still remember he was an artist who painted scenes of African villages. The quality of his art was such that it is said he later went on to design a postage stamp for his native country.

"Daddy Caines," as he was sometimes affectionately called, had a profound influence on the lives of many a youngster in old Tiger Bay. Dignified in his posture, I still recall seeing him walking down Bute Street with his walking cane, as many an African did in those days, with a shiny silver object at its tip. Certainly not a man who should be forgotten. His and the effort of others in the past had shown that facilities can be provided for youth of all ages in our community. We may have lost one generation of talented youth to the street, do we really have to lose the next?

At her home in Cathays, his Viennese-born widow Suzanne Caines keeps on display many of her late husband's works of art. Among them is a montage called the "History of Africa" which superimposes images of ancient Egypt, Moorish civilisation, the Tsetse fly that kept European imperialism at bay and a likeness of Mother Africa herself. Also among her treasured possessions is a life-like bust of Stewart Martin Caines, a man once dedicated to the youth of old Tiger Bay.

With the 1960s demolition came the final demise of the George Cross. In its place the council proposed to build the Butetown Community Centre in Loudoun Square. Initially, the loss was not apparent but soon made itself evident as the new and promising centre, now under the jurisdiction of the council, lacked the multi-purpose facilities provided by the old George Cross. This inherent design flaw gradually contributed to the fragmentation of the community as pensioners and youngsters vied for its use. From this point on, the legendary cohesiveness of the old community, which had made it such a unique and magnetic place, was put under strain.

Looking further back, prior to the turn of the twentieth century, the exportation of black gold from the South Wales valleys out of Cardiff Docks and the colourful name Tiger Bay had put Wales on the world map. Many a foreign seaman succumbed to the charms of this unique community and settled down, as did many a researcher following in their footsteps, including anthropologists and academics like Kenneth Little and friend and colleague of Ghanaian Pan-Africanist Kwame Nkrumah, the aforementioned St Clair Drake who arrived in Tiger Bay during the 1940s. By the time of the Second World War people used to say: "You could see the world in one square mile in Tiger Bay." And this was certainly true. Years later, having been a student of Drake, African American anthropologist Glenn Jordan was also drawn to our community to continue in the tradition of his mentor's earlier research.

Although the idea of collecting the local histories of Tiger Bay and the Docks had been on the community agenda for many years, the Butetown History & Arts Project, as a formal group, came into existence in 1988. Prior to this time, Jordan had become acquainted with members of the community like Olwen Watkins, Nino Abdi, Rita Delpeche, Marcia Brahim Barry, Vera Johnson, among others.

During that time Jordan assisted local residents in their desire to form a community history group which met initially for three or four years in the Butetown Community Centre and obtained offices in St Paul's Church, both in Loudoun Square. With the help of the community and Jordan's ability to attract outsiders like visual artist Beverley Morgans and computer wiz Marco Gil-Cervantes, this hard working and dedicated group collected treasured photographs from local families, made video and audio recordings of its elder members and developed an extensive audio and video archive.

In subsequent years, BHAP published such books as: *In the Shadow Of The Steelworks* by Anne Eyles with Con O'Sullivan; *Old Cardiff Winds* by Mike Johnson; *The Tiger Bay Story* by myself; *A Tiger Bay Childhood:Growing Up in the 1930s* by Phyllis Grogan-Chappell; *How I Saw It: A Stroll Thro' Old Cardiff Bay* by Harry "Shipmate" Cooke, *Cardiff and the Spanish Civil War* by Dr Rob Stradling; and *'Down the Bay': Picture Post, Humanist Photography and Images of 1950s Cardiff* by Glenn Jordan.

Now renamed Butetown History & Arts Centre, its stated ambition is, and always was, to establish a "Bay People's Museum & Arts Centre," designed to maintain and promote the unique history of this once fascinating former maritime community, at a permanent location within the area. BHAC also seeks to become a major visitor attraction in the new Cardiff Bay. Its successful photographic exhibition *People & Places of the Old Bay,* which took place in the summer of 1995, was intended as a step in that direction. This exhibition was held at the Pilotage House, a building on Stuart Street which is itself steeped in historical mystery, as no one knows when it was actually built. Some conjecture that, before it became the Pilot Office, the Marquis built it as a stable for the horses that pulled the coal trucks along the rails or the barges on the canal. It has subsequently become a series of restaurants the latest of which is *Woods Brasserie.*

Be that as it may, to keep the community and the world abreast of its activities, the first edition of Butetown History & Arts Centre's quarterly magazine *The Voice Of The Tiger* was published in 1994. Before the final edition came out in the winter of 1997, it had gained international acclaim with literary contributions arriving from such places as Australia, South Africa and the Caribbean.

However, it was made clear in January 1995 that it was not appreciated by all. During that month, a series of death threat letters were mailed without postage to prominent members of the community. One was received by *Butetown History & Arts Centre* addressed to the editor of *The Voice Of The Tiger*, referring to the magazine as "Voice of the Nigger." The anonymous author referring to himself as a "Welsh person — not a Nazi" — wrote:

> I object to the portrayal of negroes in the newsletter of the Butetown History & Arts Centre. Blacks have their own countries in Africa and should return there. Certainly, they have no business here. These people will be aliens in the land no matter how long they stay. If I go to Africa for one million years, will that make me a nigger? By the same principle, blacks, Asians and the assorted racial trash now threatening to bastardise our pure racial stock are entitled to absolutely nothing. Therefore I would thank you not to follow the Hollywood pattern by making heroes out of them. There are Welsh heroes. Let us hear about them. Be careful not to show us any niggers in future; such an action is an affront to all of us who desire a Welsh leader and the continuance of the Welsh as a distinct people-group in their own right.
>
> I sincerely hope that you are an English man because it would not give me pleasure to kill a fellow Welshman, even a traitor to race and nation.

Bequeathing such racist rhetoric to posterity, the misguided author of this shameful diatribe, evidently ignorant that this *is* nazi propaganda, clearly does not expect to find himself among the future heroes of Wales. The "nigger" in question, whose photograph was on the front page of the second edition, was Mende seaman James Roberts, the proud African great-grandfather of Manchester United footballer Ryan Giggs. In any event, Wales can also be extremely proud of its three Afro-Celtic divas in the entertainment world: Mabel Mercer, Shirley Bassey and Iris Williams.

For the record, as Peter Fryer's *Staying Power: The*

History of Black People in Britain indicates, there were black people in Britain before the English, as early historical evidence indicates an African presence among the legions of the Roman Empire who built Hadrian's Wall. However, there is provocative evidence of an even earlier multi-cultural presence among the Celtic peoples of the British Isles, indicated in Lorraine Evan's *Kingdom of the Ark* and in *The Black Celts: An Ancient African Civilization in Ireland and Britain* by Newport-born Somali author Ibrahim Ali. Co-authored with his brother, Ahmed Ali, this work scours the *Ancient Annals of Ireland* compiled by the Four Masters, which details the ancient tribes of Ireland, for evidence of the arrival of African sea-pirates known as the Formorians. The Ali brothers' attempt at uncovering a multi-cultural past among the Celts is reinforced by *The Atlanteans*, a controversial four-part television documentary by Bob Quinn, which retraces north African sea voyages out of the Mediterranean up the French coast and on to Ireland. The series uncovered musical and other cultural influences from the north African

Mende seaman James Roberts, who appeared on the cover the Winter 1994 edition of The Voice Of The Tiger, with his daugters Vera and Winnie. The latter standing to his left is the grandmother of the Manchester United footfballer Ryan Giggs. (Photo courtesy of Vera Johnson)

coast still evident among the Celtic peoples of the coast of western Europe up to the western shores of Ireland.

However, contemporary black people do not need ancient history to justify their existence in Britain. This should be evident from the ultimate sacrifice some local people, described herein, made to British society as a whole — in addition to the contributions made by other black and ethnic minority communities throughout the land. But, in contrast with those other communities, we express no strong allegiance to things black and have thus not formed a potent Afro-Celtic identity: "We're from the Bay!" or "from the Docks!" End of story.

To people from other, more homogeneous black communities like Brixton or Harlem, for example, Blacks from Cardiff — Tiger Bay and the Docks, that is — appear strange and less confident about the issue of black self-awareness. Naturally, the riots in Notting Hill during the 1950s and the development of the Civil Rights and Black Power movements in the United States during the 1960s had an effect on people of African origin in the Bay. This expressed itself in the formation of the Black Alliance in the 1970s, which coincided with the rise in martial arts taught locally by Von Johnson and musician Robert Taylor. Inspired by students from the University of Wales, who felt it necessary to ally themselves with the oldest non-white community in Wales, the Black Alliance movement raised the spectre of a pseudo-black nationalism in the youth of that time which was at odds with members of the older generation. By the 1970s and 1980s, the majority of the local youth, regardless of the wide variety in their ethnic origin, had cultivated Jamaican accents. The *Casablanca* night club in Mount Stuart Square became dominated by the sound of Reggae after Bob Marley had sounded the clarion call.

Returning home from UCLA during the mid 1970s with a Masters Degree in African Area Studies, I made a contribution to this smouldering mileux by organising the African Citadel, which delivered a series of lectures on the history of Africa in the living rooms of some members and in various other locations in the community, including the Vestry of St Mary the Virgin Church. Among that group were the aforementioned proponents of the martial arts, Markie Boy's son Clifton, Clayton Georges and the *Casablanca* DJ John Grey, father of athlete Paul Grey. However, as I have said elsewhere:

> Tiger Bay ... never was a black community. From the beginning it was always a multi-racial and intra-cultural community. In Tiger Bay there were no all-black schools or institutions. When community members point homeward to the lands of their ancestral forefathers, with feet firmly planted in Celtic soil, they point to Egypt, Yemen, Arabia, Somaliland (Somalia), Sierra Leone, Nigeria, Malta, Cape Verde, Spain etc., and needless to say the islands of the Caribbean.[2]

Obviously the people of this community as a whole have been familiar with the nuances of many black cultures. Yet, as the product of a unique history, not having experienced extreme social ostracism within the confines of its own society below the bridge, black people native to this area of Wales, with few exceptions, have never truly been hungry for a black identity separate from their multi-ethnic community.

Whereas the *Butetown History & Arts Centre*, since the 1980s, has been documenting the memoirs of the elder members of the old Tiger Bay and Docks communities, Race Equality First, in the early 1990s (when it was known as the Race Equality Council), undertook the Goal Project. This project researched the ethnic minority communities of South Glamorgan to determine if and why these communities were underrepresented in the take-up of community care services provided for the elderly by the social services. Whatever the general failings of Race Equality First, this was a useful study.

During the same period, amid much fanfare and newspaper publicity, a day centre for the elderly was proposed by the South Glamorgan County Council to be built on Bute Street, behind Loudoun Square, with support from Cardiff Bay Development Corporation. Local resident the late Beaty Murrell, who was assistant treasurer of the Butetown Community Centre at the time, said: "We are behind it 100 percent because it's something we have been fighting for over a number of years. Pensioners in Butetown currently use the community centre..."

Referring to the inadequacy of the Butetown Community Centre, which had over the last thirty years shown preference to one group over another, and excited by the prospects of the new day centre recommended for building near the shopping centre on Bute Street, Mrs Murrell said: "It will be the best thing for youngsters as well, if it gets the go ahead as they are reluctant to attend the [community] centre because of the room taken up by the elderly."

However, the elderly are still waiting as the £340,000 allegedly set aside by CBDC in 1993 never materialised. Moreover, this was not the only instance in which CBDC abandoned the community to its fate. *Twenty-Twenty Vision*, the forward plan of the Cardiff Bay Community Trust, reiterated a statement from the development corporation's *Regeneration Strategy,* published in 1988, which said that consideration should be given to the establishment of a Trust with "... community leaders as Trustees playing a significant part in long term development." In 1996 this proposal reemerged in the Corporation's consultative document in order to "... avoid a sudden vacuum in public sector support [to voluntary groups]" and to "ensure that adequate financial resources are put aside for the ongoing support of such groups."

In its document *Sustaining Success*, the Corporation gave consideration to the proposal that a sum of £2 million be made available to support its suggestion of a Trust. The Trust did not receive a £2 million endowment injection when the Corporation ceased, although it did work in the hope of receiving a substantial sum.

The purpose of the Trust was "to address the social and community concerns which remain in the Bay. The unemployment rate of young men between 16 and 19 is over 50%, and is little less among young women. 20% of the unemployed are below the age of 24. Over 25% of the population are from black and ethnic minorities for whom disadvantage is compounded by discrimination. A high incidence of long term illness prevails together with low skilled occupations. Much remains to be done in the area." Thus the support that the Corporation might have brought was a welcome addition to the discussion of the likely success of a Community Trust in Cardiff Bay.

The idea of a Community Trust had been a matter of considerable interest within the community for some long time. Among the members of the trust from Tiger Bay and the Docks were Anthony Brito, Father Shore of the Catholic Church of St Cuthbert, Betty Campbell, and Neil Sinclair. In addition, as the trust would incorporate the whole area of Cardiff Bay, other members also included Paul Morrissey, manager of NewEmploy Wales, the late Anne Goss of Willows High School, Bill Vaughan and a representative of Fitzalan High School, among others. After the initial meeting at Mount Stuart Primary School in January 1997, this Steering Group worked extremely hard for over two years on plans for the Trust and visited other trusts and took advice from many quarters. It also undertook a detailed risk analysis which proved both reassuring and encouraging.

However, within the first nine months the members of the Trust saw the initial £2 million drop to £200,000 and dwindle down to £8,000 by mid 2000 as the Development

Corporation drifted away from its initial promise. Inevitably, CBDC's failure to support the community trust means future decisions in the community will continue to be made *for us* as usual, leaving us to flounder as a community under threat.

In any event, during the years prior to this let down, the Goal Project instituted by the Race Equality Council had defined the unmet needs of the elderly in the multi-cultural community of South Glamorgan — which prompted the local authority to provide a one-off pump priming amount of £50,000 to set up Multicultural Crossroads. This organisation, based on the national respite care group Crossroads, would establish a culturally sensitive respite care service, which matched the culture and ethnicity of the service user with a carer from the same background. Much of the money was used to renovate a dilapidated betting shop on Maria Street, turning it into offices and to hire a coordinator and care staff. However competing with large local authorities for home care services for multicultural clients created many difficulties, particularly as no further funding was available from social services and three lottery applications had been rejected. As chair of Multicultural Crossroads I sounded the alarm at a conference organised by the Commission for Racial Equality in 1999 and held at Allied Steel and Wire. As no support came, I also raised the alarm at the second of such conferences entitled *A Policy and Planning Seminar on Black & Minority Elder Care Services in Wales* held at the National Assembly at Cathays Park in October 2000. Discussion at the latter conference was about the uptake of social services in the multi-ethnic community and how they had failed thus far and what was needed to be done. Naina Patel, Director of the Policy Research Institute on Aging and Ethnicity, produced a report called *Hope & Care: Black and Minority Ethnic Elders in Wales* whose proposals suggested that fourteen multi-cultural day centres for the elderly be created in Wales.

As funding for Multicultural Crossroads was defined as

a local government issue and therefore outside the jurisdiction of the CRE and the National Assembly, the question was raised: whether ninety-year olds, who were born in Tiger Bay and have seen hard times and better times in terms of multi-ethnic relations than exist today and still live there, can expect to see one of the fourteen multi-cultural day care centres for the elderly in their community? The response from Dr Mashuq Ally, Head of CRE Wales, was less than encouraging and completely out of touch with community sentiment. He said that the community must expect to be removed from its traditional home in about *two years time*.

As has already been stated, the greatest danger to the community is its own belief that we are to be bulldozed out of our homes in the interests of "Europe's most exciting water-front development." But when the opinion of the head of a multi-ethnic organisation such as CRE is like this we recognise we are on our own again and must defend ourselves. Instead of standing at the forefront in defence of the community, we find a highly paid multi-cultural executive administering the final demise of the *colony* — expecting the community to surrender to the worst excesses of venture capitalist development, like those perpetrated in the Third World, committed here on our doorstep.

Thus, according to the very organisation set up to protect the interests of ethnic minorities, the old Tiger Bay community probably faces imminent demise. If this is all the support the community can expect from such an organisation as the CRE then, mark my words, as in 1919, barricades will be raised and petrol bombs will be at the ready as the new millenium progresses. That this will not be necessary, we live in hope.

ENDANGERED TIGER

EPILOGUE

"For thirty years we've been a long time dying."

Keith Murrell

Today there is a conspiracy theory making the rounds among the multi-ethnic residents of Tiger Bay and the Docks. Gaining momentum among some residents is a belief that there is a hidden strategy to destablise what remains of the Tiger Bay community — the final *coup de grâce*. For some this occult scheme, perpetrated by the powers that be, manifests itself as a deliberate policy of *flooding* the community with newcomers and refugees, who have no stake in the history of the locale. Prior influxes over the years have never overwhelmed this community. However the current fear is that people are being brought in in large numbers whose roots lie elsewhere and who will readily move to other parts of the city when the time comes so that this seafront land can be usurped for further upmarket housing developments. This seems a rational paranoia.

At times I have shared the pessimism and apathy that many in the community have felt over the years. After all, the people of this community have lived on a building site since the 1960s demolition, which radically disrupted a century or more of familiarity and stability. Thus the deeply-rooted community perception that the Cardiff Bay Development Corporation was created to finish off what the council failed to do during the 1960s: *get rid of Tiger Bay!*

Nevertheless, prior to the departure of the development corporation, Cardiff County Council created a scheme — the Butetown/Grangetown Strategy — to improve the otherwise neglected areas of Butetown and Grangetown, but its effectiveness is yet to be measured.

Since the demise of CBDC, Cardiff County Council has taken over the reigns of the continuing development of South Cardiff following the less than spectacular ceremonial departure of its predecessor in the spring of 2000. However, had the development corporation been given the remit at the beginning of its inception to upgrade the miniscule area of Tiger Bay and the Docks, in all likelihood, this gesture would have caused less anxiety in the community.

Sadly, Cardiff Bay Development Corporation's demoralising failure to support the *community trust* that it had a statutory duty to implement in the wake of its exit strategy has ignited a cultural implosion. This has manifested itself in the community's sense of abandonment: the closure of NewEmploy Wales and the subsequent loss to the community of its much appreciated local magazine *Making Waves*; the closure of Multicultural Crossroads, and the downsizing of Tiger Bay Community Arts, resulting in the demise of the annual carnival are some of the main features of this internal collapse. In the first year of the new millennium there was no carnival.

Discouragingly, after more than twelve years of development, we still have the highest unemployment rate in Wales. Since the closure of the docks and the industries surrounding them, unemployment has remained chronic and the under-utilisation of talented people in the area remains a social crime. And if circumstances are not depressing enough, some in the community believe that we are going to be bulldozed out of our traditional area and that the Butetown council estate will be torn down. However, such a possibility will not be as easily accomplished as it was in the 1960s.

Some external detractors with misguided voices comment that 98% of the people in the area are on benefits and are basically living in rented accommodation. The fact, however, is that many own their own homes and flats on the estate — as had been the case in the old community.

In addition, as outlined earlier in chapter two, even in this new millennium the print media still cling on to their outmoded descriptions of the area. In "Charlotte's Secret," an article published on 18 March 2002 in the *Daily Mail,* reporters Tara Conlan and Adam Lee "dig the dirt" on Wales' latest international singing sensation Charlotte Church: our community is described derogatively in their report as "the docklands of Cardiff where drugs and prostitution are rife." RIFE! More like rampant journalism running rife. That these intrepid reporters actually stumbled over an abundance of those sirens of the night within the confines of "Europe's most exciting waterfont development," seems truly a most unlikely scenario! Nevertheless, the apparent purpose of this latest attempt at defaming Tiger Bay is to embellish in sordid detail the waywardness of Charlotte's choice of boyfriend: a lad of Tiger Bay descent who, incidentally, belongs to the same family that produced boxer Steve Robinson. Seventeen-year-old Rap DJ Steven Johnson, whom she is allegedly dating, is said to be "dark and swarthy" and from a "crime-torn council estate," even though his family home stands in the shadow of the world-class St David Hotel & Spa — an area which, in reality, has an extremely low crime rate and forms an integral part of the new Cardiff Bay.

Although located in the Docks and not Tiger Bay, his family home is further described as a "two-bedroom council house in the graffitti-covered Tiger Bay docklands area of Cardiff." According to these reporters, many of the friends he grew up with had allegedly "fallen foul of the law for offences linked to drugs, theft and petty car crime." The article refers to Johnson as penniless compared to the millions possessed by Charlotte, implying thereby that he is out of her league, for she after all has travelled the world "playing to audiences including the Pope and Bill Clinton." This article fails to take into account that, long before her international fame, Charlotte was not unfamiliar with the local community where she appeared at cabaret concerts organised by the late Sy Scott at the Butetown Community Centre in the heart of old Tiger Bay. Known locally as Benny Mohammed, cabaret artist Sy Scott of old Nelson Street helped to promote Charlotte in the early days of her career. Taking into account that the popular press needs these kinds of stories to boost sales, clearly it will take some time for London-based newspapers to catch up with the changes that have taken place in and around this area of the world.

Without the industrial docks the remnants of our seagoing community would have inevitably perished in the absence of some sort of development. Thus, for all its failings, in relationship to the community of Tiger Bay and Docks, Cardiff Bay Development Corporation and its successor body holds out the best prospects for its future. With the government offices of the National Assembly for Wales on our threshold, perhaps there is a hope that even these shortcomings may be resolved.

"Tiger Bay" is the most famous name in Wales and Bute Street, world renowned long before Shirley Bassey was born in it in 1937, the most famous address. Yet since the 1960s' attempt at social engineering, disguised as redevelopment, there has been a gradual dissipation of the name Tiger Bay in favour of "Butetown" — which even some residents have gradually taken on aboard. It seems that the price for that reputation to improve in the South Wales press has been the acceptance of the name "Butetown," superceding the more colourful "Tiger Bay." And in *So Sinks Tiger Bay*, Beatrice Sinclair poignantly remarked: "Now Tiger Bay is called Butetown." The fact is that prior to the 1960s' demolition, residents either lived *up the Bay* or *down the Docks* and letters were addressed to the Docks and Butetown as a name was hardly, if ever, mentioned in the community. While the debilitated Tiger cowers under the shadow of Cardiff Bay, communities like Newtown, Adamsdown, Splott and Tremorfa continue to exist under the new development's umbrella without having to give up their identities. Rather than let the name Tiger Bay fall into oblivion, should it not be officially recognized in some manner as Drake, Columbus, Scott and Lloyd George have been recognised in the nomenclature of Cardiff Bay? With the exception of the latter, their only relationship to the port of Cardiff is that they had something to do with the sea, as did all our forefathers in the community. Perhaps at least a bus stop somewhere in the area could have the title Tiger Bay?

Ironically the name Tiger Bay had been seriously considered as a possible choice for the name of the new development. However, according to Neil Sullivan's unpublished dissertation, the name *New Tiger Bay* "proved too nostalgic for some and the more acceptable Cardiff Bay was adopted."[1]

Furthermore, the Cardiff Bay Development Corporation displayed a certain degree of arrogance when it did not deem it important to consult any residents in the community when it officially changed the name of Bute Street railway station to Cardiff Bay. Indeed, no aspect of the community's Tiger Bay past was utilized by the development corporation in its promotion of the new *sanitized* image that Cardiff Bay was to represent. This suggests a need for a conservation trust for the survival of an endangered Tiger — one that showed an ethnically-fragmented world, for more than a century, that people from different ethnic groups could live together in harmony.

With regard to multi-culturalism, Tiger Bay will remain Britain's beacon of the twentieth century for years to come. Some, however, have already read our obituary. Thus a recent January 2002 article in Cardiff County Council's *Capital Times* begins with the statement "Once known as Tiger Bay..."

My take on that is this: like others of my generation and older, I was born in Tiger Bay and every night I sleep in Tiger Bay and for me it will remain Tiger Bay. After I die, you can call it what you want.

Ultimately, we may be the last genuine community in the city where people still know who their neighbours are and this is the reason I love it and believe there is a future worth fighting for.

NOTES & REFERENCES

NOTES

Preface

1 Whenever the term "Docks" is capitalized, it is a reference to the people of the residential district only. Lower-case spelling refers to the actual working docks.

Chapter One

1 Davies, John: *Cardiff and the Marquis of Bute*, University of Wales Press, 1981, p. 18.

2 Sullivan, Neil: Unpublished dissertation: *From Tiger Bay ... to Cardiff Bay, 150 Years of Socio-economic Change in Butetown*, Bristol Polytechnic, 1990, p. iii.

Chapter Two

1 Details of this story from my mother's memories are given in more detail in *The Tiger Bay Story* and in the play produced by Made In Wales in 1997: *Tiger Bay Moonshadows*.

2 For the interpretation of the media presentation of this case, I am indebted to the efforts of Maidy Jalil, a student in a course I taught in 1995 on "Race, Discourse and the Media" at the University of Glamorgan.

Chapter Three

1 Evans, Neil: "Immigrants and Minorities in Wales," *Llafur, Journal of Welsh Labour History*, no. 4, vol. 5, 1991, p. 14.

2 Sinclair, Neil M. C.: *The Tiger Bay Story*, Cardiff, Butetown History & Arts Project, 1993 and Dragon & Tiger Enterprises, 1997, p. 53.

3 Green, Jeffrey: *Black Edwardians, Black People in Britain 1901-1914*, London, Frank Cass Publishers, 1998, p. 61.

4 Ibid., p. 61.

Chapter Four

1 Green, Jeffrey: *Black Edwardians*, London, Frank Cass Publishers, 1998, p. 60-61.

2 See The Tiger Bay Story, p. 69.

3 Ibid., p. 34.

4 Although Muriel Burgess' *Shirley: An Appreciation of the Life of Shirley Bassey* showed her birth certificate, I find many people still believe that she was not born in Tiger Bay.

Chapter Six

1 Evans, Neil: "Immigrants And Minorities In Wales," *Llafur, Journal of Welsh Labour History*, no. 4, vol. 5, 1991, p. 10.

2 Ibid., p. 10.

3 Green, Jeffrey: *Black Edwardians*, p. 66.

4 Evans, Neil: "Immigrants And Minorities In Wales," p. 15.

5 Behan, Brendan: *Borstal Boy*, London, Arrow Books, 1990, p. 251.

6 Ibid., pp. 353-354.

7 Ibid., p. 361.

Chapter Eleven

1 Green, Jeffrey: *Black Edwardians*, p. 148.

2 Sinclair, Neil M. C., *The Tiger Bay Story*, p. 129.

NOTES

Epilogue

1 Sullivan, Neil: Unpublished dissertation: *From Tiger Bay ... to Cardiff Bay, 150 Years of Socio-economic Change in Butetown*, Bristol Polytechnic, 1990, p 68.

REFERENCES

Ali, Ibrahim & Ahmed Ali: *The Black Celts, An Ancient African Civilization in Ireland and Britain*, Cardiff: Punite Publications, 1992.

Bamford, Joe: *The Salford Lancaster: The Fate of 106 Squadron's PB304*, Barnsley: Pen & Sword Paperbacks, 1996.

Behan, Brendan: *Borstal Boy*, London: Arrow Books, 1990. (First published in the United Kingdom in 1958 by Hutchinson & Co. Ltd.)

Burges, Muriel: *Shirley: An Appreciation of the Life of Shirley Bassey*, London: Century, 1998.

Davies, John: *Cardiff and the Marquises of Bute*, Cardiff: University of Wales Press, 1981.

Evans, Lorraine: *Kingdom Of The Ark, The Startling Story Of How The Ancient British Race Is Descended From The Pharaohs*, London: Simon & Schuster, 2000.

Evans, Neil: "Immigrants And Minorities In Wales," *Llafur, Journal of Welsh Labour History*, no. 4, vol. 5, 1991.

Fryer, Peter: *Staying Power, The History of Black People in Britain*, London: Pluto Press, 1984.

Green, Jeffrey: *Black Edwardians, Black People in Britain 1901-1914*, London: Frank Cass Publishers, 1998.

Sinclair, Neil M. C.: *The Tiger Bay Story*, Cardiff: Butetown History & Arts Project, 1993 and Dragon & Tiger Enterprises, 1997.

REFERENCES

Sullivan, Neil: *From Tiger Bay ... to Cardiff Bay, 150 Years of Socio-economic Change in Butetown*, Unpublished thesis, Department of Surveying, Bristol Poloytechnic, 1990.

Local Magazines

The Voice of the Tiger: The Official Newsletter of Butetown History & Centre, Nos. 2, 4, 5, 6, 7, (1994-1997).

Making Waves in the Bay, a publication of NewEmploy Wales, Issue no. 91, April 1998.

About The Author

Neil Sinclair is a native son of the Tiger Bay community. Although he spent over two decades in the United States, this absence served only to intensify his interest in his roots. Particularly since his birthplace experienced a complete transformation during the early 1960s, his desire to record for posterity to the best of his ability the true essence of the life lived in his community is his life-long ambition.

He graduated with a Masters' Degree from the University of California at Los Angeles and gained his Bachelors' Degree from the same university at Berkeley.

Since his return to Cardiff at the beginning of the 1990s, he has written *The Tiger Bay Story* and *The Cardiff Bay Experience*. In addition he produced a video entitled *A Stroll Through Tiger Bay* which was the culmination of a decade-long series of history walks. Negotiating with the Cardiff Bay Development Corporation to sponsor these walks. he was able to offer them to the general public free of charge. The Open University has also recorded his history walk and regularly airs this program on television.

As a recognized source of information on the life and times of the community of Tiger Bay, he is often seen in the media discussing his favourite subject.